Java Manual
of Style

JAVA MANUAL
OF STYLE

Nathan Gurewich
and Ori Gurewich

Ziff-Davis Press
an imprint of Macmillan Computer Publishing USA
Emeryville, California

Development Editor	Kelly Green
Copy Editor	Mitzi Waltz
Technical Reviewer	Robert McDaniel
Project Coordinator	Barbara Dahl
Proofreader	Ami Knox
Cover Illustration and Design	Megan Gandt
Book Design	Gary Suen
Technical Illustration	Sarah Ishida
Word Processing	Howard Blechman
Page Layout	M.D. Barrera
Indexer	Valerie Robbins

Ziff-Davis Press imprint books are produced on a Macintosh computer system with the following applications: FrameMaker®, Microsoft® Word, QuarkXPress®, Adobe Illustrator®, Adobe Photoshop®, Adobe Streamline™, MacLink®Plus, Aldus® FreeHand™, Collage Plus™.

Ziff-Davis Press, an imprint of
Macmillan Computer Publishing USA
5903 Christie Avenue
Emeryville, CA 94608
(510) 601-2000

ISBN 1-56276-408-X

Manufactured in the United States of America
10 9 8 7 6 5 4 3 2

Contents at a Glance

TABLE OF CONTENTS

Part 2   Programming with Java

Part 3   Java Examples

ACKNOWLEDGMENTS

We would like to thank Stacy Hiquet, Publisher, who asked us to write this book. Many thanks to Kelly Green, Development Editor of this book. We would also like to thank the other people at Ziff-Davis Press who contributed to the development and production of this book: Mitzi Waltz, Copy Editor; Barbara Dahl, Project Coordinator; and Robert McDaniel, Technical Editor.

Finally, we would like to thank the people at Sun Microsystems who designed the Java product and made it available to the Internet world.

INTRODUCTION

What is Java? And why is everybody talking about it? In *Java Manual of Style* we'll answer these questions, and then we'll show you how to design and implement Java programs yourself to take advantage of this exciting new technology.

As you can guess, the Java programming language, which was created by Sun Microsystems, has nothing to do with coffee. (Rumor has it that the people involved with creating a name for this new programming language thought of it while visiting a coffee shop during their lunch break.) Java can enhance your HTML pages with animation, sound, and other programs such as games, graphics, interactivity, and everything else that you may think of. Java enables you to create HTML pages with a great deal of programmability.

> **Note:** Why is coffee called java? In 1690, Dutch mariners smuggled coffee plants from the Arab port of Mocha and planted these plants in one of their colonies. The name of that colony was Java; hence the association between coffee and java.

The Internet is a very powerful means for connecting millions of computers. Many types of computers communicate through this giant network of networks; some people use a PC with the Windows 3.1*x* operating system, others use a PC with Windows 95, still others work with the UNIX operating system, and so on. Naturally, it would not be a good idea to create a segregated computer society where people with Windows 95 could only communicate with people that had Windows 95, UNIX users could only communicate with other UNIX users, and so on. On the Internet, no matter what computer you have, you're able to communicate with all other types of computers.

This was the idea behind HTML. An HTML page is a text file that contains code. This code enables your computer to extract information from remote computers working on any platform through the Internet's World Wide Web. An HTML-coded Web page can contain pictures, text, and hyperlinks to other documents on the Web. The text can be in different colors, different sizes, and different fonts.

To read these Web pages, your computer must have a program called a Web browser. Your Web browser will establish communication with other computers that are connected to the Internet by requesting the HTML text file from the remote computer and displaying it as a page on your monitor. The thing to note here is that the HTML page looks the same to all computers—a regular text file that contains information. Your browser will read and interpret the contents of the HTML file, and will display it on your computer's monitor. So in addition to the actual information that is included in the HTML file, the HTML file also contains instructions of how to display the information.

As you can imagine, the HTML file should not contain data that is unique to a particular computer or operating system, because the remote computer does not know the type of computer that will receive the HTML file. The fact that HTML is accessible to all platforms greatly limits the capabilities and sophistication of the HTML page. For example, suppose that you want to design a HTML page that includes animation. If you are familiar with a programming language such as Visual Basic or Visual C++, you probably know that creating such a program is not a complicated task. But creating such a program and embedding it inside a HTML file *is* a complicated task, because the HTML page must work on any platform. When an animation program is executed over the Internet on your computer, the program utilizes the resources of your computer. Because the way these resources are used differs from one operating system to the next, it simply isn't possible write a "universal" animation program that can be executed on any computer.

So how was the problem of creating animation programs inside Web pages solved? Quite simply, the people who designed the HTML protocol do not allow the inclusion of animation, or any other feature that does not work on multiple platforms, in the HTML standard.

Animation is just one area in which HTML's capabilities are limited. Another area is the integration of sound into an HTML page. Currently, you can use HTML to download a sound file from a remote computer to your computer. Once the sound file is downloaded, you can use software on your computer called a helper application to play the sound. But with HTML alone you can't, for example, create a page where several pictures are displayed and, depending on where your mouse cursor is located, a different sound file is played automatically.

Some ingenuous ways to accomplish some limited animation and sound playback were invented using CGI technology. A CGI program resides on the remote computer and performs some sophisticated tasks that HTML alone can't handle. However, the fact that the CGI program resides on the remote computer is a major limitation, because to do the simplest task a lot of data has to flow from the remote computer to your computer over the modem. This, of course, makes the process of executing CGI programs relatively slow.

Java actually lets you embed programs directly inside your HTML pages. In this book we'll show you how to design Java programs and embed these programs in your HTML pages, and you'll also see some of these Java programs in action.

Here's how Java works with HTML and your Web browser to execute a program in your Web page. First, your Web browser downloads the HTML text file and notices that the HTML contains a Java tag. So the browser also downloads the Java program that is indicated by the tag. Then the browser executes the Java program. Unlike CGI, where the program resides on the remote computer, Java programs are downloaded directly into your computer and executed by your browser. So while the initial download time for a Java program may be long, once it resides on your computer it runs just as fast as any other program on your local hard drive. And Java programs are written in such a way that they work exactly the same way regardless of computer platform.

Not all Web browsers are equipped to to handle Java, which is still a new concept. Netscape Navigator 2.0 is an example of a browser that is Java-enabled. Sun Microsystems, the company that developed Java, also has a Java-enabled Web browser, called HotJava; however, the final version of HotJava has not yet been released, and as of this writing it does not support the current release of Java.

Part 1

Java: The Solution to Powerful Web Programming

Java: What Is It? Who Needs It?

Discovering Java with the Java
   Developer Kit

Java: What Is It? Who Needs It?

Quick review: The Internet, the Web, and more

Java to the rescue

Platform independence

What is a Java-enabled Web browser?

How this book is organized

Java is fun!

I n this chapter you'll learn what Java is, why you would want to use it, and why it's so popular.

Java is a programming language that is used in connection with the Internet. So before proceeding to the topic of Java, let's quickly review some basic Internet topics that are prerequisites for utilizing the material in this book.

QUICK REVIEW: THE INTERNET, THE WEB, AND MORE

To understand why Java is so important and so powerful, you must first understand current Internet technology and the limitations of this technology. As you'll soon see, Java is merely a natural evolution of these technologies: a language that enhances current Internet and World Wide Web capabilities.

When using the Internet, you are basically connecting your PC to a remote computer, or a network of remote computers, that may offer a variety of data including image files, sound files, movie files, programs, or advertisements.

The program that you need on your PC to accomplish communication over the Internet's visually oriented World Wide Web is called a *Web browser*. Your Web browser transfers data to your PC from the remote *Web server*, reading the text, graphics, and other files that are combined to make Web pages. There are many Web browsers available; Netscape Navigator 2.0 is one of the best known.

Your Web browser displays the data that you receive via the Internet on your monitor. When you download files, for example, it saves the downloaded files to your hard drive. Let's take a look at the data that will be displayed on your screen. Server computers you encounter on the Internet will not know which platform you are using, so how can you be sure they will send data that can be displayed on your monitor? To ensure easy access to information on the World Wide Web, most Web-page designers have adopted a popular data format called Hypertext Markup Language, or HTML.

THE CAPABILITIES OF HTML-BASED WEB PAGES

Hopefully you have browsed through sections of the World Wide Web before, and seen some of the wonderful and impressive Web pages that can be constructed using HTML. One of HTML's built-in features is the ability to add hypertext links to Web pages. Web-page authors use hypertext to make links to other Web pages and files, usually as text that is underlined and/or a different color. When users click on the underlined text the hypertext link is activated, transporting them to another Web page or carrying out some other function. For example, a Web page might contain the text <u>Click me to view more information</u>. When the user clicks this text, the remote Web-page server receives an indication that the client (the user's PC) has activated the hypertext link, and then it sends a new Web page to the client. The user's Web browser then displays this new Web page on his or her monitor.

What else can you accomplish with hypertext links on Web pages? You can also set up links that will automatically display another section of the same Web page when clicked. This feature is typically used when the Web page is too long to fit on a single screen.

HTML also supports codes (called *tags*) that let you specify the background color for the window where a Web page is displayed, the color of the text, and a variety of other cosmetic features. You can even place buttons, text boxes, check boxes, and radio buttons inside a Web page. For example, if the page presents the user with check boxes and the user places a check mark inside one, the Web server will receive an indication that the user checked the check box and can be instructed via CGI coding (see "CGI Scripts" later in this chapter) to undertake a certain operation. Check boxes, radio buttons, list boxes, and edit boxes can be used as a mechanism for getting input from users, and then sending that data from the user's computer to the Web server.

Hypertext links on Web pages can also be attractively presented as part of a picture, or *image map*. The user has to click the appropriate part of the picture to display a different Web page.

However, that's all HTML can do: just present data and take in data in a cosmetically pleasant way. Although you can place buttons or image maps inside your Web page, they can do little more than put a different interface on the same hypertext operations you can accomplish with simple text links.

DOWNLOADING FILES FROM A REMOTE WEB SERVER

Web pages can also be set up to let users download files from a remote Web server. For example, if a user clicks the text **Load the Game Program**, the HTML code on the page can be written to cause the server (or another linked computer) to send a file to the user. The user's Web browser will then let him save the file on his machine's hard drive.

SOUND AND MOVIES

In the previous section you learned that Web pages can be used for downloading programs from a remote server. In the same manner, they can let users download sound files and movie files. When the user's Web browser discovers that a downloaded file is a sound file or a movie file, it lets the user either save the file or open a program that can play the sound or run the film clip.

These programs that work with specific types of downloaded data are called *helper applications*. For example, Media Player is a program for PCs running Windows that lets users play certain types of sound and video files. If the user has instructed her Web browser to work with Media Player, it will automatically play downloaded files.

CGI SCRIPTS

Obviously, HTML has many features that let you design Web pages that are both elegant and functional. But a Web page created with HTML is not a computer program. A computer program is a set of statements that lets you accomplish some task—and the beauty of programming is that there are no limitations or restrictions on the type of tasks that a program can do. A program can perform complex calculations, display a sequence of pictures with simultaneous sound, and handle many other complicated tasks. With HTML alone, you do not have the opportunity to perform programming tasks via Web pages.

There is a way to add some limited programmability to Web pages created with HTML. This is accomplished with Common Gateway Interface, or CGI, scripts. To understand CGI scripts, consider a Web page that includes an edit box. The edit box lets the user type text within its borders. Suppose also that the same page includes a button that the user is expected to click after typing text in the edit box. What happens when the user clicks the button? The text will be sent to the remote server. And what will the remote server do with the text? The remote server will execute a CGI program that will do something with it. For example, the text could be e-mailed to the owner of the remote server, allowing users to send questions and suggestions to a central location.

Naturally, the CGI script program must reside on the remote Web server's hard drive, so any programs it triggers run on that machine—not the user's.

THE LIMITATIONS OF HTML

The World Wide Web is becoming so popular that new features are constantly being thought up to make Web pages more attractive, and to add more advanced features to HTML. HTML 3.0 includes features that further enhance the capabilities of HTML. Naturally Web browser software must also evolve to keep pace with these changes.

But even with these new HTML specifications, HTML-based Web pages are very limited when it comes to performing programming tasks. In short, HTML is not a programming language; it is merely a script that lets the Web browser present data, much like the PostScript language that word processing software uses to format documents for the computer screen or for printing.

JAVA TO THE RESCUE

Java is a programming language created by Sun Microsystems that lets you enhance the programming capability of HTML when designing Web pages. Suppose you wanted to design the following Web page using HTML:

- The Web page will display a picture of a cartoon character.

- When a user clicks anywhere within the window of the page, the cartoon character will "walk" toward the point where the mouse was clicked. In other words, when a user clicks inside the window, an animation show will be performed.

- To make the animation show more interesting, a sound file will be played as the cartoon character "walks" toward the point where the mouse was clicked.

Currently, the preceding program specifications cannot easily be implemented using HTML. If you have written programs with Visual Basic, Visual C+, or any other programming language, you probably know that this program would be a relatively simple thing to write. But with HTML, it is impossible.

Experienced HTML designers will probably tell you that the window where the page is displayed could be divided into many little squares, each one a separate image with its own hyperlink. When a user clicks on a certain area of the Web page, the server sends out another page hyperlinked to that particular square, showing the cartoon character in a different position from before. As this process continues the user receives many consecutive Web pages, giving the illusion of the cartoon character moving to the point where the mouse was clicked.

What about the sound? As stated earlier in this chapter, when a sound file is sent to the client, the Web browser lets the user either save the sound file to his hard drive, or play the sound file. Again, experienced HTML writers and Web browser users will tell you that there is a way to eliminate the need for a dialog box that offers this choice, instead forcing the user's Web browser to immediately play the sound file.

Your intuition may have already told you that the preceding "solution" is the wrong way to make the animation show happen. It requires the server to transmit many Web pages to the user's PC, a process that takes time and processing power. The animation will not be smooth, and users will hardly notice that an animation show is going on. In fact, you'll probably only succeed at annoying the user!

While the preceding "solution" requires a lot of ingenuity and many Web pages, it results in poor performance. By using Java, you can implement the program with great ease, and get a solution that will please users with high performance and fewer demands on their time, hardware, and patience. Basically, that's what Java is all about: enhancing the programming capability of HTML so that Web pages will be able to execute programs.

How do you incorporate a Java program into a Web page? As you'll soon see, it's just a matter of using a tag (a code inside the HTML script that defines the page) that specifies the name of the Java program to be executed. In essence, using Java does not alter the way you currently use HTML. Just as the <HR> tag causes a Web browser to display a horizontal line, another tag will cause the execution of the Java program that you design and write. Naturally, the <HR> tag serves a single purpose: displaying a horizontal line. Each Java tag is also specific, executing one Java program.

To enhance your Web pages, all you have to do is use the proper HTML tag syntax. It's the same with Java—except that you can write a Java program that performs just about any task you want it to perform. In fact, when writing Java programs, don't think of Java as an Internet-related programming system. Java is just like Visual C++, Visual Basic, or any other programming language. The beauty of Java is that you can execute programs written in it using HTML tags within Web pages.

Remember that program that moves a cartoon character to the point where the user clicked her mouse? At first glance, it might sound like a silly program—

but think about it! Animation is a great way to attract a user's attention. As you know, using the Web has become a popular way to advertise all sorts of products. With HTML, the advertiser can display attractive pictures. By adding Java technology, the advertisement can be made even more eye-catching and interactive.

However, advertising is just one of many applications for Java. Java lets you write Internet programs that perform like other state-of-the-art, powerful programs on your PC. You can write games, educational software, programs that perform complex mathematical calculations, and so on.

Remember, the essence of the HTML-based Web page remains the same. That is, you can still use hypertext to move the user from one page to another. And each Web page can contain its own Java program. Now you can understand why so many people were very excited when Sun Microsystems announced the development of Java.

PLATFORM INDEPENDENCE

In fact, you might be wondering why something like Java was not implemented earlier. People have been willing to consider enhancing HTML, which has gone through three versions now, to make its performance as a page-description language more sophisticated. Why weren't their efforts directed toward the implementation of a programming language embedded inside HTML? It seems like a natural evolution of today's Internet technology, and as the Internet has become more popular, implementing "programmable HTML" has indeed become a very desired feature. However, implanting a programming language like Java within HTML is not an easy task!

Why? Because Web servers have to serve clients (users) that could be using IBM PCs running the Windows 3.1x, Windows 95 , Windows NT, or OS/2 operating systems; computers with the Unix operating system or Apple Macintosh machines. In other words, the server must be able to handle multiple platforms, so Java or any similar programming language must be designed in a way that also works on any computer. This is quite a challenge, but Sun Microsystems has finally succeeded.

WHAT IS A JAVA-ENABLED WEB BROWSER?

All Web browsers can read HTML files and display the Web pages they describe accordingly. Each HTML tag gives a different instruction to the Web browser, telling it how to display the Web page. Remember that a new tag must be added to an HTML Web-page description to specify which Java program to execute. Because Java programming is still new, many existing Web browsers do not understand the tags that specify the execution of Java programs. And when a Web browser encounters a tag that it cannot interpret, it simply ignores the unknown tag—hence, your Java program will not be executed by most Web browsers. Of course, as Java gains popularity, more and more Web browsers will support it. (See Chapter 2 for more details.)

To encourage you to test and experiment with Java programs, Sun Microsystems has developed AppletViewer, a small utility program that lets you execute Java program outside the context of the Web page. During the course of this book, you'll have a chance to experiment with this important tool.

NO PREVIOUS C OR C++ EXPERIENCE NECESSARY!

If you have previous C or C++ programming experience, you'll notice that the Java programming language is very similar to these languages. However, if you don't have previous C or C++ programming experience, don't worry—it's not essential for using this book.

HOW THIS BOOK IS ORGANIZED

By the time you complete this book, you'll be able to write your own Java programs and incorporate Java programs into your HTML Web pages.

In Chapter 2 you'll learn how to download a copy of Java from the Internet. You'll also learn how to execute sample Java programs that come with the Java software. This way, you'll be able to see some Java programs in action right away.

In Chapter 3 you'll write your first Java program, and you'll incorporate it into an HTML-based Web page, following these steps:

- ▸ Writing the Java program

- ▸ Compiling the Java program

- ▸ Incorporating the Java program into your Web page

- ▸ Viewing the Web page with your Java program embedded in it

Java is a regular programming language. You can use conditional statements such as If…Else, loops, and all the other programming building blocks that you find in other languages. In Chapter 4, you'll learn how to use these programming building blocks in Java. You'll do so by writing small Java programs that perform if checking, loops, and other basic computing operations.

One of the main features of Java is its ability to play sound files. Unlike a regular Web page that only lets you download a sound file, you can write a Java program that lets the user click a button to automatically play a sound file. In Chapter 5 you'll learn how to incorporate sound into your Java programs.

Another important feature of Java is its ability to incorporate graphics and images. In Chapter 6 you'll learn how to display images and graphics with Java.

In Chapter 7 you'll learn about threads and multitasking, extracting tag values from an HTML-based Web page, and working with animation.

Note: When you write a Java program, your end user may be the person who views the Web page that has the Java program you designed in it. In other words, you may write Java programs for the sake of designing your own powerful and impressive Web pages. Another reason for designing Java programs is helping other people design sophisticated Web pages without needing to program with Java. You can design your Java programs to include some degree of programmability, such as the ability to play any desired sound file. Your end user in this case would be a person who designs Web pages but does not want to bother with Java.

In Chapter 8 you'll learn how to incorporate standard user interface mechanisms, such as buttons, into your Java programs.

In the Quick Reference you'll find more important information, such as how to search for additional Java-related data and software and reference material that can help you extend your Java programming abilities.

JAVA IS FUN!

The bottom line is that Java is fun! Don't forget that the main reason Java was designed is to make Web pages prettier and more powerful. Java was not designed to help launch a spaceship toward the moon. It's meant for playing sound over the Internet, putting animation online, improving user interfaces on the Web, and things of that nature. So relax, and prepare yourself for a very pleasant Java journey.

Note: Although Java is a language that functions on all platforms, we have used the Windows 95 environment for our examples throughout the book. If you are working on a different platform, please keep in mind that some basic conventions and commands differ from platform to platform.

Discovering Java with the Java Developer Kit

DOWNLOADING THE JDK

SEEING IS BELIEVING... TESTING THE
  POWER OF JAVA

VIEWING SAMPLE APPLETS IN THE
  DEMO\ANIMATOR DIRECTORY

OTHER EXAMPLES OF JAVA APPLETS

I n this chapter you'll learn about the Java Developer kit (JDK), a set of software tools that will let you develop Java programs. You'll also see what you can do with Java by examining some sample applets that came with the JDK. In Chapter 3, you'll learn how to develop Java applets and embed these applets in your HTML page.

DOWNLOADING THE JDK

We are in the global information age, so getting information is easy. Of course, the ease with which you can get information over the Web depends very much on the provider of that information. Luckily, Sun Microsystems has made its Java products available on its Web site. In addition to JDK, Sun offers press releases, documentation, sample programs, and everything else you'll need to look over as you study the Java language.

As you probably know, Web sites are very dynamic in nature, so don't be surprised if the data that you find while you're surfing the Sun Web site differs from what we have described below.

SURFING THE SUN WEB SITE

Use your Web browser to access the Sun Microsystems Java Web site at the following URL:

```
http://java.sun.com/
```

An ocean of information is now at your fingertips! You can spend hours finding out about every aspect of Java. For now, however, just make sure to download the Java software as follows:

1 Log into the http://java.sun.com/ page of the Sun Microsystems site. This Web site lets you link to other Java-related pages in the Sun Web site.

2 Look for the link to the page that lets you download the Java Developer Kit.

3 When you find the Web page that lets you download the JDK, scroll down the window until you see the following hypertext:

```
Download the JDK for
            SPARC/Solaris 2.3, 2.4, or 2.5
            Microsoft Windows NT/95
```

Click on *Download the JDK.*

4 The Download Instructions page appears. Click on the link that corresponds to the operating system you are using. For example, if you are using Windows 95, click on

```
Microsoft Windows NT and Windows 95
```

5 Keep following the instructions until you've downloaded the JDK. Make sure to read them carefully. Use your Web browser's printing feature to print the instructions for installing Java on your computer; you will need them when the download is complete.

Note: In this chapter, we'll assume that you're running Windows 95.

EXPANDING THE JDK JAVA PACKAGE
The file you downloaded from the Sun site is a self-extracting executable file. Copy this file to your C drive, then expand it. Several subdirectories will appear:

> C:\Java

> C:\Java\bin

> C:\Java\demo

> C:\Java\include

> C:\Java\src

The C:\Java\bin directory Inside the C:\Java\bin directory you'll see several files. The most important files are Java.exe, JavaC.exe, and AppletViewer.exe.

Java.exe is the interpreter program; an *interpreter* is a program that can execute Java programs. JavaC.exe is the Java compiler; a *compiler* is a program that converts the text code of your program to a binary program that the computer can run. AppletViewer is a program that lets you view your Java work.

SETTING THE PATH AND THE HOME ENVIRONMENT VARIABLE

The C:\Java\bin directory contains several programs that you'll need during the course of this book, so you first need to establish a path to the C:\Java\bin directory:

1 Open the C:\Autoexec.bat file with your text editor. If for some reason you do not have the Autoexec.bat file in your C directory, then use your text editor program to create the C:\Autoexec.bat file.

2 Edit the Autoexec.bat file so that the DOS path includes the C:\Java\bin directory. To do this, add the following line to the end of the Autoexec.bat file:

```
PATH = C:\Java\Bin
```

3 After this line, add the following line at the end:

```
set HOME=C:\
```

This statement sets an environment variable called *HOME* to the C root drive, which is where Java was installed. If you created a new Autoexec.bat file, it should look like this:

```
PATH = C:\Java\Bin
SET HOME=C:\
```

4 Save the modified Autoexec.bat file into the C root directory.

5 Exit Windows and restart your PC. (It is necessary to reboot your computer for the new Autoexec.bat file to take effect.)

TESTING THE PATH AND HOME VARIABLES

Before proceeding, let's make sure that the PATH variable is set correctly and that the HOME variable is set to C:\. First, click the Start button for Windows 95, then select the MS-DOS Prompt item from the list of programs that appears. Windows 95 will respond by executing DOS. Then, at the DOS prompt type **PATH** and then press the Enter key. DOS will respond by displaying the path as follows:

```
C:\Windows;C:\Windows\Command;C:\Java\Bin
```

Note that because Windows 95 is running, the C:\Windows and C:\Windows\Command directories will be automatically added to the path. The C:\Java\Bin directory was also added to the path because you included the PATH statement in your Autoexec.bat file.

Now let's see if the HOME variable is set correctly. At the DOS prompt, type **SET** and then press the Enter key. DOS will respond by displaying various SET settings. One of these settings should be

```
HOME=C:\
```

This setting was implemented because you added it to your C:\Autoexec.bat file.

Now exit from DOS and return to Windows. At the DOS prompt, type **EXIT**, and then press Enter.

Now Java is ready: You can start developing Java programs. You'll begin by executing some sample Java applets. Then, starting with Chapter 3, we'll show you how to write your own applets.

SEEING IS BELIEVING... TESTING THE POWER OF JAVA

Beginning with Chapter 3, you'll start developing Java applets by yourself. But first, let's practice by executing some sample applets that came with the JDK. This will show you what Java is all about, what it can do, and what type of Java applets you can develop on your own.

VIEWING SAMPLE APPLETS IN THE DEMO\ANIMATOR DIRECTORY

One of the subdirectories that was created when you installed the JDK is the C:\Java\Demo directory. In this directory you will find some very interesting Java applet samples. Let's see some of these samples in action:

1 Execute the DOS program from Windows 95.

2 Make sure that you have a path to the C:\Java\Bin directory (which you created earlier in this chapter). This is necessary because you are going to execute the AppletViewer program, which resides in this directory.

3 At the DOS prompt, type the following DOS command:

```
CD C:\Java\Demo\Animator
```

Then press Enter. This command sets the current directory to the
C:\Java\Demo\Animator directory.

4 At the DOS command line, type

```
AppletViewer Example1.html
```

Then press Enter. This command tells the AppletViewer to execute the
Example1.html file, and the AppletViewer displays the applet shown in
Figure 2.1.

Figure 2.1: The Example1.html page inside the Animator directory

The AppletViewer does not display the Example1.html page; it only displays
the applet that is embedded inside the Example1.html file. (You'll learn how to
embed applets inside HTML pages in subsequent chapters.)

If you have Netscape Navigator 2.0 or another Java-enabled browser, you
can actually view the Example1.html page. When the Example1.html page is
viewed with Netscape Navigator, the window shown in Figure 2.2 is displayed.

The Example1.html applet plays an audio file and displays an animated
sequence.

OTHER EXAMPLES OF JAVA APPLETS

Inside the C:\Java\Demo\Animator directory you will also find two other Java
applet demos, Example2.html and Example3.html. Follow the same technique
you used to execute the Example1.html page to execute these. For example, to
execute the Example2.html page, make sure you are logged into the
C:\Java\Demo\Animator directory, and at the DOS prompt type the following
command:

```
AppletViewer Example2.html
```

Then press Enter. If your Web browser is Java-enabled, you can use it to view
the Example2.html page.

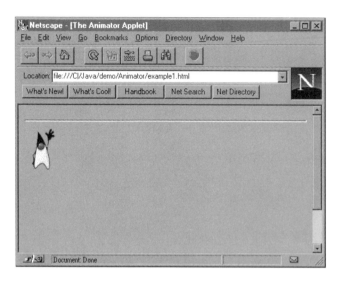

Figure 2.2: Viewing the Example1.html page with Netscape Navigator 2.0

The C:\Java\Demo directory contains many other samples as well. For example, in the C:\Java\Demo\MoleculeViewer directory, Example1.html displays the molecular structure shown in Figure 2.3. You can change this structure by dragging parts of the image with your mouse. In other words, this is an example of an applet that lets the user change graphics with the mouse, a capability that does not exist in HTML pages without Java technology.

It is highly recommended that you examine a few of the other examples provided with the JDK inside the C:\Java\Demo directory. As you execute additional examples, you'll soon realize that with Java you can do a lot of sophisticated programming. In fact, Java is a "regular" programming language that enables you to write graphics, audio, animation, user interface, and other programs.

> **Note:**   As you go over these examples, keep in mind that Java is a new programming language. Be warned that you may come across some bugs during the execution of the examples. One annoying problem that you may discover is the noticeable delay before images are displayed. Whenever you execute an example that displays images, be patient, because it may take some time for images to load.

The rest of this book will give you the skills you need to create your own Java applets. The applets you'll develop won't be as complex as the examples in the C:\Java\Demo directory. However, each applet we'll discuss demonstrates a

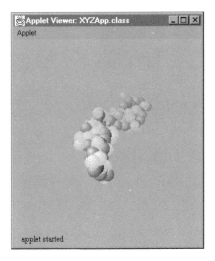

Figure 2.3: Using Java to generate and view graphics

particular Java programming application: You'll learn how to implement
audio playback, implement graphics, display images, implement animation,
create buttons and list boxes, detect mouse clicking, display strings, and other
tasks. After you've learned how to use Java to handle these basic operations,
you can build on your new capabilities to develop much more complex and
unique applets.

Part 2

Programming with Java

Creating Applets and Applications with Java

WRITING AN HTML PAGE THAT UTILIZES AN APPLET

USING THE APPLETVIEWER PROGRAM

CREATING YOUR FIRST APPLET

CREATING APPLICATIONS WITH JAVA

I n this chapter you'll learn about applets, and you'll also learn how to embed applets inside an HTML page and how to execute them. Then you'll learn how to create Java applications that are executed with the Java interpreter.

An *applet* is a program code that you can embed inside an HTML page. As discussed in Chapter 1, without Java applets the HTML page lacks the power to execute programs. With applets, your HTML can perform calculations, animation, multimedia, interactive operations, and more.

WRITING AN HTML PAGE THAT UTILIZES AN APPLET

Note: Before you read further, create a subdirectory called MyDemo under your C:\Java directory. The applets you develop during the course of this book will be saved to this directory. Then create a subdirectory within MyDemo called MyHello for this lesson.

Before you start creating Java applets, you'll need to create an HTML file in which to embed the applet. So first, create a new document in your text editor (you can use Notepad or Wordpad), and enter the following text into the document:

```
<html>
<title>MyHello.html</title>
<body>
```

```
<h1>This is the MyHello.html page.</h1>

<applet code=MyHello.class width=150 height=150>
</applet>

<hr>
This HTML page uses the MyHello.class applet.
<hr>

</body>
</html>
```

Name this file *MyHello.html*, and save it as a regular text file inside the C:\Java\MyDemo\MyHello directory.

If you use a Web browser to display the MyHello.html file, you'll see the page shown in Figure 3.1.

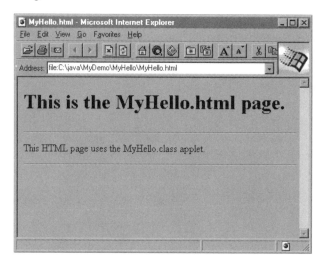

Figure 3.1: The MyHello.html page

Compare the contents of the MyHello.html text file with Figure 3.1. The browser displays the MyHello.html page as dictated by the MyHello.html file, except for the following tag:

```
<applet code=MyHello.class width=150 height=150>
</applet>
```

This tag tells the browser to execute an applet called *MyHello.class*. When you specify the name of an applet, the file extension of the applet is *class*. So the syntax for specifying an applet inside HTML page is as follows:

```
<applet code=name and size of the applet>
…
… other parameters of the applet
…
</applet>
```

Note that you can specify various parameters for the applet. For example, in the applet tag that you embedded inside the MyHello.html file, you specified the width and height of the applet (in units of pixels). So the graphical area of the applet is a square that is 150 pixels by 150 pixels. You can display text, draw lines and pictures, and so on inside this graphical area.

So why didn't the browser execute the applet tag as specified in MyHello.html? Because you did not write the MyHello.class applet yet. When the browser does not find the applet file, it ignores the applet's tag.

Next we'll create an applet called MyHello.class.

USING THE APPLETVIEWER PROGRAM

Because Java is still a new concept, most Web browsers cannot handle the applet tag. That is, even if you created the MyHello.class applet, most browsers would not be able to execute it. This means that you must use a browser that can handle applet tags.

One browser that can handle applet tags is HotJava. HotJava was developed by Sun Microsystems, and you can download it from the Sun Web site. Netscape Navigator version 2.0 and above also handles applet tags.

Sun has provided with its developer's kit a program called AppletViewer, which lets you execute your applets without a Web browser. You can find this program, called AppletViewer.exe, inside your C:\Java\Bin directory. Here's how you can use the AppletViewer program to view your applets:

1 Exit to a DOS shell, make sure that you have a path to the C:\Java\Bin directory, and then log into the C:\Java\MyDemo\MyHello directory.

2 At the DOS prompt, type

```
AppletViewer MyHello.html
```

and then press Enter. AppletViewer tries to execute the MyHello.class applet, and the window shown in Figure 3.2 appears.

Figure 3.2: Executing the MyHello.html page with the AppletViewer program

3 AppletViewer does not display the entire HTML page; only the applet is shown. However, because you have not yet created the MyHello.class applet, at the bottom of the window shown in Figure 3.2 the following message appears instead of the applet:

```
start: applet not initialized
```

4 Select Quit from the Applet menu to terminate the AppletViewer program.

Next, we'll create the MyHello.class applet.

CREATING YOUR FIRST APPLET

To create your applet, you will start by creating a regular text file with your text editor. The file extension of this text file will be *.java* (for example My-Hello.java). Inside this text file you will type the code of the applet, which you will write using the Java programming language.

Once you save the Java file, you have to compile it. The Java compiler creates a class file from the Java file. For example, when you supply the My-Hello.java file to the Java compiler, the compiler creates a new file called MyHello.class file. This new file is called the *class file*.

The process of compiling Java files to create class files with the Java compiler is shown in Figure 3.3.

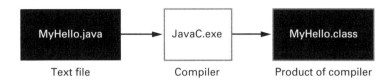

Figure 3.3: How the compiler works to create a class file from a Java file

CREATING THE MYHELLO.JAVA FILE

Now you'll create the MyHello.java file. Create a new document in your text editor. Inside the document, type the following:

```
// MyHello.java

import java.awt.*;
import java.applet.*;

public class MyHello extends Applet
{

  public void paint(Graphics g)
  {

  g.drawString("This is a test",0,50);

  } // end of paint()

} // end of MyHello class
```

Name this file MyHello.java, and save it in the C:\Java\MyDemo\MyHello directory.

> **Note:** Java code is case sensitive, so don't forget to capitalize words exactly as shown above. (For example, type MyHello rather than MYHELLO or Myhello.)

Before discussing this code, let's compile the MyHello.java file. In other words, let's create the MyHello.class file.

From Windows, execute a DOS shell, verify that you have a PATH to the C:\Java\Bin directory, log into the C:\Java\MyDemo\MyHello directory, and at the DOS prompt type

```
JavaC MyHello.java
```

and press Enter. Remember to type the *.java* file extension in lowercase and enter the file name exactly as shown here (in other words, MyHello.java, not MYHELLO.java). This DOS command causes the JavaC compiler to create the MyHello.class file.

SEEING THE MYHELLO.CLASS APPLET IN ACTION

Now that you've created the MyHello.java file, used the JavaC.exe compiler to create the MyHello.class applet, and created the MyHello.html file that contains the MyHello.class applet tag, you're going to use the AppletViewer program to execute the MyHello.class applet.

From a DOS shell, make sure you have a path to C:\Java\Bin, log into the C:\Java\MyDemo\MyHello directory, and at the DOS prompt type

```
AppletViewer MyHello.html
```

Then press Enter. AppletViewer responds by displaying the window shown in Figure 3.4.

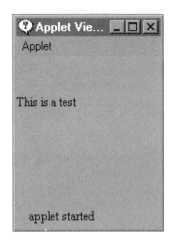

Figure 3.4: The MyHello.class applet executed with the AppletViewer

The text *This is a test* appears in the window shown in Figure 3.4. Note that the AppletViewer displays only the applet, not the entire html page.

If you have a Web browser that is capable of viewing Java applets, you can load the MyHello.html file into your browser to see the applet work—that is, display the text *This is a text*—inside the page.

How MyHello.java works   The MyHello.class applet is a very simple applet; all it does is display the text *This is a test.* Let's go over how the code of My-Hello.java works to display this text.

At the beginning of the MyHello.java file you typed the following:

```
// MyHello.java
```

This is called a comment. *Comments,* which are preceded by two forward slash marks, are totally ignored by the JavaC compiler. In other words, everything that is typed after the // characters on the same line is not compiled. Here is an example of a comment:

```
// This is my comment.
```

You could have also typed the following comment:

```
//////////////////
// MyHello.java //
//////////////////
```

> **Note:**   In Java, you can spread a statement over more than one line. For example, the following two statements are identical:
>
> ```
> MyInteger =3;
> ```
>
> and
>
> ```
> MyInteger =
>          3;
> ```
>
> Each of these two statements sets the value of a variable called MyInteger to 3. Spaces are also ignored by the Java compiler. Thus, all of the following statements are identical:
>
> ```
> MyInteger = 3;
> MyInteger =  3;
> MyInteger =   3;
> MyInteger =    3;
> MyInteger =     3;
> MyInteger =      3;
> MyInteger      = 3;
> MyInteger     = 3;
> MyInteger    = 3;
> MyInteger = 3;
> ```

Importing reusable code   After the comment, you typed the following statements inside the MyHello.java file:

```
import java.awt.*;
import java.applet.*;
```

These two statements tell Java to use code that was already written and prepared, or *reusable code.*

　To discover the origin of this reusable code, first take a look inside the C:\Java directory. One of the subdirectories is C:\Java\lib. One of the files inside the C:\Java\lib directory is classes.zip. (You do not have to unzip the classes.zip file yourself—Java is capable of extracting the code from the zipped file.) Unzipping the classes.zip file creates the new C:\Java\lib\classes subdirectory. The classes subdirectory itself has various subdirectories, including C:\Java\lib\classes\java\awt. Inside the C:\Java\lib\classes\java\awt directory you see many files with the .class file extension. The C:\Java\lib\classes\java\applet subdirectory also contains several .class files. In other words, when you installed the Java package, various classes were copied to the Java subdirectory. These .class files can perform various operations. Consider these files gifts from Sun Microsystems to make your programming job easier. That is, Sun has supplied all the basics for writing a powerful applet, and all you have to do to use the preprepared code is simply use the appropriate *import* statements.

> **Note:**   In Java, you must terminate a statement with a semicolon.

Declaring the MyHello class   Next in the MyHello.java file you declared the *MyHello* class. You did this by entering the following text:

```
public class MyHello extends Applet
{

...
code of MyHello class
...

} // end of MyHello class
```

The first line declares the name of the class. The actual code of the class is enclosed by curly brackets ({}).

　The first line of the class declaration starts with the keywords *public class.* This means that a class is being declared. The word *public* means that the class can be used from within other classes (in other words, you are making the class available for other classes). After the word *public* you typed the name of the class, which is *MyHello*.

CLASSES AND OBJECT ORIENTED PROGRAMMING

Note that after the name of the class in your MyHello.java document are the words *extends Applet*. To understand the meaning of this phrase, you have to understand that Java is an object oriented programming (OOP) language. (Other examples of OOP are Visual C++, Visual Basic, and Delphi.) This means that the programs you write and design are composed of *objects*, such as buttons, scroll bars, and applets.

Let's say, for example, that you want to implement a button in your applet. Implementing a button from scratch is a process that takes a very long time to develop. You have to draw the button, set the size of the button, set the caption of the button, write code that will be executed whenever the user clicks the button, draw the button in its down position whenever the button is pushed down, and implement a variety of other tasks to make the button operational. That's a lot of work! This is where object oriented programming comes to your rescue. Instead of forcing you to design and implement the button from scratch, object oriented programming provides you with a class. The class contains all the basic and fundamental code that you will need for the object you want to implement. Then, to implement a specific button in your program, you'll create an object that is based on this basic button. This button you create *inherits* all the code that the button class contains. However, from within your program you'll also be able to customize the button object; for example, you will need to set the caption and perhaps the size of the button. But most of the code that your button object needs is already available in the button class.

As you can imagine, writing an applet from scratch is even more complicated and requires more development time than implementing a button from scratch. Java designers don't expect you to implement applets from scratch, so they designed the *Applet* class. This is the reason you typed the import statement to import the classes that reside inside the C:\Java\classes\Java\Applet subdirectory. When creating new applets, you are basing your new applets on the Applet class. You are telling Java that the MyHello class is an applet that is an extension of the Applet class by using the keywords *extends Applet*.

The paint() method Inside the MyHello class you typed the *paint()* method as follows:

```
public void paint(Graphics g)
{
```

```
...
... Here you type the code of the paint() method
...

} // end of paint()
```

To understand the paint() method, you have to understand the mechanism by which Java programs are executed. When the Web browser (or the Applet-Viewer) encounters the applet tag, it starts executing the applet mentioned in the applet tag—in our example, the MyHello.class applet. When the MyHello applet is executed, the paint() method is also automatically executed.

A *method* is a block of code that is executed on a class. As its name implies, the paint() method paints the applet. For example, if inside the paint() method (or, more specifically, inside the curly brackets of the paint() method) you write code that draws a cat, upon the execution the MyHello.class applet a cat will be drawn. In your applet example, you typed code that displays the text *This is a test*.

Let's take a look at the first line of the paint() method. You preceded the name of the paint() method with the keywords *public void*. *Public* means that you are making the paint() method available to other classes. *Void* means that the paint() method does not return any value. But let's say you wanted to write a method called *Calculate()* that performed the calculation of multiplying the number x by the number y; then the first line of the Calculate() method might look like this:

```
public int Calculate(int x, int y)
{

return x*y;

{
```

In this case you would not use *void* as the return value, because you would want Calculate() to return an integer that is the result of multiplying x by y. Inside the parentheses of the Calculate() method you would type *int x, int y*: These are the *parameters* of the Calculate() method. The job of the Calculate() method is to return the result of this multiplication. The appearance of the word *int* preceding x and y indicates that they are integers.

Why doesn't the paint() method return a value? And why is *Graphics g* the parameter of the paint() method? One reason is that you don't have any choice in the matter. Recall that the MyHello class is an extension of the Applet class, which already has the paint() method in it. By including your own paint() method inside the MyHello class, you essentially tell Java to *override* the original paint() method—that is, you are forcing Java to execute the paint() method that you typed inside the MyHello class. But when you override a method, you must maintain the same returned value and parameters that the original method had. This is why your customized paint() method has *void* as a returned value and *Graphics g* as its parameter.

If you compare *Graphics g* with *int x* of the Calculate() method, you'll see that *g* is a name of a variable. Unlike *x*, which is a variable of type *int*, *g* is a variable of type *Graphics*. You know that *x* is capable of holding integers. What can the *g* variable hold? Because *g* is of type *Graphics*, it can hold data that represents the graphical area.

Now let's take a look at what you typed inside the paint() method:

```
g.drawString("This is a test",0,50);
```

This statement applies the *drawString()* method on the *g* variable. (Note that there is a dot separating the *g* from the drawString() method.) Java automatically executes the paint() method and supplies *g* as the parameter of paint(). As a programmer, you don't really care about the value of *g*; rather, you care what *g* represents. In the case of the paint() method, Java automatically set *g* with a value that represents the graphical area of the applet. In other words, *g* represents the area of the applet where you can draw lines, print text, and do other graphical operations.

The drawString() method draws the string that is listed as the first parameter of the drawString() method. The result is that the text *This is a test* is drawn inside the applet area. The second parameter of the drawString() method represents the vertical distance between the upper edge of the applet's area and the place where the text is drawn. Because you supplied *0* as the second parameter, the text will be drawn starting at the left side of the applet area. The third parameter of the drawString() method represents the horizontal distance from the left edge of the applet area. Because you supplied *50* as the third parameter, the text will be drawn 50 pixels below the top edge of the applet's area. The result is shown in Figure 3.4.

More about the paint() method   When our sample applet is executed, the paint() method is executed—or, more precisely, the paint() method is automatically executed whenever there is a need to repaint the applet's area. For example, when the applet is first executed, the applet's area needs to be drawn. The applet's area needs to be redrawn if the user

▶ Hides the applet's area with another window and then removes the other window

- ▸ Minimizes and then restores the size of the applet's window
- ▸ Drags the applet's window outside the monitor area and then drags the window onto the screen again

In all of these cases, the paint() method is automatically executed, because Java recognizes that the applet's area needs to be repainted.

CREATING APPLICATIONS WITH JAVA

So far, we've only discussed applets (programs that you embed inside HTML pages). But can you write a "regular" application with Java? In other words, can you write an application that does not need an HTML page to run? The answer is yes. In addition to applets that you embed inside HTML pages with the Applet tag, you can also write Java applications that can be executed outside an HTML page.

In the following example you'll learn how to write a simple Java application called MyHelloApp. You will then execute the MyHelloApp application without the AppletViewer and without the use of a HTML page.

The process of making a Java application is very similar to that of making an applet. You create the source code of the program with a regular text editor program, and then you save the source code as a regular text file with *.java* as its file extension. This process is shown in Figure 3.5.

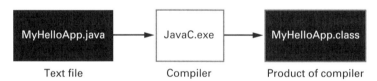

| MyHelloApp.java | JavaC.exe | MyHelloApp.class |
| Text file | Compiler | Product of compiler |

Figure 3.5: Making an application with Java

You use the same Java compiler for applications as you do for applets—JavaC.exe. The JavaC.exe program works on the MyHelloApp.java file to create a new file called MyHelloApp.class. You can then execute the MyHelloApp.class file with the Java interpreter, a program called Java.exe that resides inside the C:\Java\Bin directory.

In this example you are going to create a Java application called MyHelloApp. The purpose of this example is to illustrate how the Java compiler (JavaC.exe) works to create Java applications, and how the Java interpreter (Java.exe) works to execute them.

CREATING THE JAVA SOURCE CODE FILE

Before you start coding, create a subdirectory within your Java directory called *MyApps*. Your Java application files will reside here.

Now let's create the MyHelloApp.java file, which is the source code of the application. Open a new document in your text editor, and then enter the following code:

```
// MyHelloApp.java

class MyHelloApp
{
    public static void main(String args[])
    {
    System.out.println("This is MyHelloApp application!");
    }
}
```

Name this file *MyHelloApp.java*, and save it inside the C:\Java\MyApps directory.

> **Note:** It is not a Java requirement to end the name of the application with App. However, it is a good idea to do so, because otherwise you may not be able to differentiate between an applet and an application.

COMPILING THE MYHELLOAPP.JAVA FILE

Now let's compile the MyHelloApp.java file. Looking back at Figure 3.5, this means that your objective now is to use the JavaC.exe program to create the MyHelloApp.class file. Here is how you use the JavaC.exe compiler:

1 From Windows, execute to a DOS shell.

2 Make sure that you have a path to C:\Java\Bin, then log into the C:\Java\MyApps directory

3 Type the following at the DOS prompt:

```
JavaC MyHelloApp.java
```

Then press Enter. Remember to type the file extension all lowercase (*MyHelloApp.java*). Otherwise the JavaC program will not recognize which file you want to compile.

4 The JavaC.exe compiler compiles the MyHelloApp.java file and creates the MyHelloApp.class.

EXECUTING MYHELLOAPP.CLASS WITH THE JAVA INTERPRETER

Now let's execute MyHelloApp.class as an application with the Java interpreter. From the DOS shell, log into the C:\Java\MyApps directory. At the DOS command line, type

```
Java MyHelloApp
```

Then press Enter. The Java interpreter (Java.exe) executes the MyHelloApp.class application, and the MyHelloApp application displays the following:

```
This is MyHelloApp application!
```

> **Note:** When using the Java interpreter to execute an application, do not type the class file extension. That is, type **Java MyHelloApp**, not **Java MyHelloApp.class**. Also, remember to type the name of the class in the proper case.

The syntax for writing a Java application is identical to the syntax for writing Java applets. For example,

- Each statement must terminate with a semicolon.

- You must declare a class and then type the code of the class inside curly brackets.

- Comment lines start with the // characters.

- Spaces are ignored by the compiler.

One of the main differences between a Java application and a Java applet is the fact that a Java application must contain a function called main(). When you execute the application, the Java interpreter program (Java.exe) looks for main().

The main() function that you typed inside the MyHelloApp class is

```
public static void main(String args[])
{

System.out.println("This is MyHelloApp application!");

}
```

This code causes the computer to print a line with the text *This is MyHelloApp application!*.

Congratulations! In this chapter you created your first applet and your first Java application. As you saw, you can create applications and then execute them with the Java interpreter (Java.exe). Typically, though, you'll use Java for creating applets, which you'll embed inside your HTML page. Therefore, the majority of this book concentrates on creating applets.

Java Programming Building Blocks

JAVA, C, AND C++

COMMENTS IN JAVA

EXPERIMENTING WITH JAVA
 PROGRAMMING BUILDING BLOCKS

LOOPS

Chapter

4

In this chapter you'll learn about the programming building blocks of Java. In the previous chapter you got your first look at Java applets. Developing applets amounts to writing code with the Java programming language. As a programming language, Java includes all the standard programming building blocks, including conditional statements, loops, assignment of values to variables, and operators (addition, subtraction, and multiplication).

Java, C, and C++

If you have previous programming experience with C or C++, you will soon realize that Java is very similar to both. However, Java is not identical to C/C++—in fact, its developers have made it easier to use. To use Java and this book, no previous C/C++ experience is assumed. Naturally, if you have C/C++ experience, you'll find the Java material much easier.

You may have heard performance comparisons between Java and C/C++. Programs written in Java are about 20 times slower than those written in C/C++. But as the popularity of Java increases, it is expected that additional enhancements and improvements will make it capable of creating faster programs.

Comments in Java

When you are writing Java programs, you may want to include comments within your program. You use the // characters to indicate a comment in the source code file (.java file) of your programs. For example, the following represents a comment:

```
// This is my comment.
```

Another way to write comments in Java is to start the comment with the characters /*, and to end the comment with */. In this case, the comment can be spread over multiple lines. The following are examples of valid comments in Java:

```
/* This is
   my comment. */

/*
This is my comment.
*/
```

Of course, you can be creative and make your comments pleasant looking:

```
/***********************\
 *                     *
 *  My comment is here  *
 *                     *
\***********************/
```

This comment is valid because the first line starts with /* and the last line ends with */.

EXPERIMENTING WITH JAVA PROGRAMMING BUILDING BLOCKS

In this chapter you'll experiment with the fundamental building blocks of Java programming. Let's first implement a simple Java applet as an experiment. Several files are needed to implement an applet. You'll now prepare the files that will be used in this chapter.

PREPARING THE HTML FILE

First we'll create the MyApplet.html file. This file will be used as your HTML page for learning and experimenting with Java's programming building blocks.

First, create the C:\Java\MyDemo\MyApplet directory. You'll save the files that you create as you work through this chapter in this directory. Then open a new document in your text editor and save it as a regular text file with the name *MyApplet.html* inside the C:\Java\MyDemo\MyApplet directory. Type the following code inside the MyApplet.html file:

```
<html>

<title>MyApplet.html</title>

<body>

<h1>This is the MyApplet.html page.</h1>

<applet code=MyApplet.class width=150 height=150>
</applet>

<hr>

This HTML page uses the MyApplet.class applet.

<hr>

</body>
</html>
```

As you can see, the MyApplet.html file utilizes the MyApplet.class applet:

```
<applet code=MyApplet.class width=150 height=150>
</applet>
```

You'll implement the MyApplet.class applet later in this chapter.

PREPARING THE JAVA FILE

You'll now create the MyApplet.java file that you'll use for experimenting with the Java programming language as you work through the exercises in this chapter.

Use your text editor program to create a regular text file called MyApplet.java, and save the file inside the C:\Java\MyDemo\MyApplet directory. Type the following code inside the MyApplet.java file:

```
// MyApplet.java

import java.applet.*;
import java.awt.*;
import java.awt.peer.*;
import java.awt.image.*;
import java.io.*;
import java.net.*;
import java.util.*;
```

```
public class MyApplet extends Applet
{


  public void paint(Graphics g)
  {

  g.drawRect(10,
             10,
             120,
             120);

  } // end of paint()


} // End of the class
```

COMPILING THE MYAPPLET.JAVA FILE

You'll now compile the MyApplet.java file. That is, you'll use the JavaC.exe program to create the MyApplet.class file from the MyApplet.java file.

Execute a DOS shell. Make sure you have a path to the C:\java\Bin directory (the directory where the JavaC.exe file resides). At the DOS prompt, type

```
JavaC MyApplet.java
```

Then press Enter.

> **Note:**   When typing this DOS command, make the M and the A in
> MyApplet.java capital letters. The rest of the characters should be
> lowercase letters.

JavaC will respond by compiling the MyApplet.java file, and if you typed the code exactly as it appears above, the MyApplet.class file will be created.

You may now use AppletViewer to see the MyApplet.class applet in action. At the DOS prompt, type

```
AppletViewer MyApplet.html
```

Then press Enter. AppletViewer will respond by displaying the window shown in Figure 4.1.

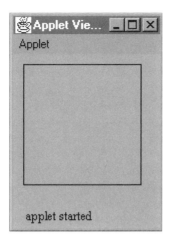

Figure 4.1: The MyApplet.class applet viewed with the MyApplet viewer program

As you see in Figure 4.1, the applet has a rectangle drawn in it. The rectangle is drawn inside the paint() method by using the drawRect() method as follows:

```
public void paint(Graphics g)
  {
  g.drawRect(10,
          10,
          120,
          120);
  }
```

You drew a rectangle inside the applet because you'll need to be able to tell where the applet's area is located. In this case, the area inside the rectangle is also the area of the applet. When using AppletViewer, the whole window of AppletViewer is the applet's area, so the rectangle is not needed. However, if you execute the MyApplet.html file with a Java-enabled Web browser such as Netscape Navigator 2.0, you'll find the rectangle to be a very good indication of where on the HTML page the applet is located.

DISPLAYING TEXT

One of the first things a programmer wishes to know when learning a new programming language is how to display text. So let's start by finding out how to display a simple line of text.

The drawString() method Here's how to display a simple line of text using the drawString method. First, use your text editor to add the following code to the end of the paint() method inside the MyApplet.java file:

```
g.drawString("Hello, I was drawn with drawString()",
             20,
             30);
```

After you add the code, the paint() method should look like this:

```
public void paint(Graphics g)
{

g.drawRect(10,
           10,
           120,
           120);

g.drawString("Hello, I was drawn with drawString()",
             20,
             30);
} // end of paint()
```

The drawString() method works on g, which represents the graphical area of the applet, to display the string *Hello, I was drawn with drawString()*.

The first parameter of the drawString() method ("Hello, I was drawn with drawString()") is the string to be displayed. The second and third parameters of the drawString() method (20,30) are the x and y coordinates of the upper-left corner of the imaginary rectangle that encloses the string being displayed.

Save the modified MyApplet.java file, then use the JavaC compiler program to compile the MyApplet.java file, creating a new MyApplet.class file. Then use AppletViewer or a Java-enabled Web browser program to execute the MyApplet.html file.

AppletViewer will respond by displaying the MyApplet.class applet, as shown in Figure 4.2. The text *Hello, I was drawn with drawString()* will be displayed inside the MyApplet.class applet's area.

Finally, select Close from the Applet menu to terminate the execution of the MyApplet applet.

The only problem with the current state of the MyApplet applet is that the area of the applet is not large enough to hold the string that you want to display with the drawString() method.

Figure 4.2: A string is being displayed inside the applet's area

One way to increase the area of the applet is by changing the parameters of the MyApplet.html file. Recall that inside the MyApplet.html file you typed the following:

```
<applet code=MyApplet.class width=150 height=150>
</applet>
```

This means that the MyApplet.class applet is inside the MyApplet.html page, and the size allocated for the applet is 150 pixels wide and 150 pixels tall. To increase the applet's area, you can set new values for the width and height parameters.

You can also increase the applet's area in a different manner, using the init() method.

THE INIT() METHOD

To increase the area of your applet, open your MyApplet.java file in your text editor, and then add the init() method as follows:

```
public class MyApplet extends Applet
{

    public void init()
    {

    resize (250,200);

    }// end of init()
```

```
...
...
...

} // End of the class
```

Increase the width of the rectangle so that the drawRect() method inside the paint() method will be as follows:

```
g.drawRect(10,
           10,
           200,
           120);
```

Use JavaC.exe to compile the modified MyApplet.java file, then use Applet-Viewer to execute the MyApplet.html file.

AppletViewer now displays the MyApplet.class applet as shown in Figure 4.3. As shown, the applet's area is larger, and the text that you display with the drawString() method fits nicely inside the applet's area. (Note that the applet's area is larger than the rectangle's area).

Select Close from the Applet menu to terminate the execution of the MyApplet applet.

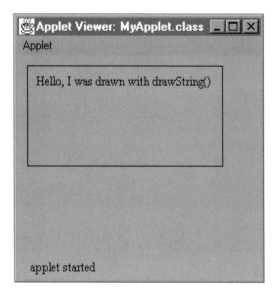

Figure 4.3: The MyApplet.class applet with its larger area

The init() method that you typed is automatically executed whenever the applet is started, so the init() method is a good place to type code that performs various types of initialization. You can type code inside the init() method that sets a new size for the applet:

```
public void init()
    {

    resize (250,200);

    }// end of init()
```

Using the resize() method inside the init() method sets the width of the applet to 250 pixels and the height to 200 pixels. In other words, the width and height settings that you indicated inside the MyApplet.html file with the applet tag will be overridden by the code that you type inside the init() method. (The applet size will change when viewed with the AppletViewer. However, when viewed with the Netscape browser, the applet will have the size specified in its tag.)

DECLARING VARIABLES IN JAVA

During the course of writing Java programs, you'll need to utilize variables. A *variable* stores various types of data—numbers, strings, and so on. But before you use variables from within your Java programs, you must tell Java the type of data represented by the variable that you want to use. Here's an example.

First, use your text editor to add the CalculateRectangleArea() method inside the MyApplet.java file after the paint() method:

```
public int CalculateRectangleArea(int a, int b)
{
    ...
    ...
    ...
} // end of CalculateRectangleArea()
```

After adding the CalculateRectangleArea() method, your MyApplet.java file should look like this:

```
// MyApplet.java

import java.applet.*;
import java.awt.*;
import java.awt.peer.*;
import java.awt.image.*;
import java.io.*;
```

```java
import java.net.*;
import java.util.*;

public class MyApplet extends Applet
{

    public void init()
    {

    resize (250,200);

    }// end of init()


  public void paint(Graphics g)
  {

  g.drawRect(10,
            10,
            200,
            120);

  g.drawString("Hello, I was drawn with drawString()",
              20,
              30);



  } // end of paint()


  public int CalculateRectangleArea(int a, int b)
  {

  int Area;

  Area = a * b;

  return Area;
  } // end of CalculateRectangleArea()


} // End of the class
```

Take a look at the first line of the CalculateRectangleArea() method that you added to the MyApplet class. The word *int* that appears after the word *public* means that the CalculateRectangleArea() returns an integer (a whole number, not a fraction or decimal). In other words, the CalculateRectangleArea() method is a block of code that does something useful: It calculates the area of a rectangle. You designed the CalculateRectangleArea() method to return the area of a rectangle, and this area must be an integer.

The first line of the CalculateRectangleArea() method also indicates the parameters of the method inside the round parentheses. The first parameter of the CalculateRectangleArea() is *int a*. This means that the CalculateRectangleArea() will work on a variable called *a*. And because you preceded the *a* parameter with the word *int*, the *a* variable must be an integer. Similarly, the second parameter of the CalculateRectangleArea() method is *b*, which also must be an integer.

If you now compile the MyApplet.java file, you'll create the MyApplet.class file. And if you then use AppletViewer to execute the MyApplet.html file, you'll see the MyApplet class in action. But you will not see the area of the rectangle. Why? Because you never executed the CalculateRectangleArea() method. Unlike the init() method and the paint() method, which are automatically executed by Java, the CalculateRectangleArea() method is not. Later in this chapter you'll find out how to deliberately execute the CalculateRectangleArea() method.

Using global variables   A *global variable* is a variable that is visible by any method. You declare a global variable at the beginning of the class declaration.

Let's add the declaration of a variable called *iArea* of type *int* to the beginning of the MyApplet class declaration. After adding this declaration, the beginning of the class declaration should look as follows:

```
public class MyApplet extends Applet
{
int iArea;
...
...
...
}
```

Now every method inside the MyApplet class can set the value of iArea, as well as read the value of iArea.

Displaying the tectangle area   Now we'll modify the code of the paint() method of the MyApplet class by adding code that displays the value of the rectangle's area.

Add the following code after the drawString method inside the MyApplet class in the MyApplet.java file:

```
g.drawString("iArea = " + iArea,
             20,
             30);
```

Now the paint() method should look like this:

```
public void paint(Graphics g)
  {

  g.drawRect(10,
             10,
             200,
             120);

  // g.drawString("Hello, I was drawn with drawString()",
  //                 20,
  //                 30);

  g.drawString("iArea = " + iArea,
             20,
             30);


  } // end of paint()
```

The code that you typed comments out the original drawString() statement. The last statement inside the paint() method is now

```
g.drawString("iArea = " + iArea,
             20,
             30);
```

This statement displays the string *iArea =* followed by the value of iArea. For example, if iArea is equal to 0, then the preceding statement will draw

```
iArea = 0
```

If you now execute the MyApplet applet, you'll see that iArea is equal to 0. Why? Because CalculateRectangleArea() still has not been executed, and iArea was not set to any particular area. In other words, you declared iArea as an integer, and you declared it at the beginning of the MyApplet class. Thus, paint() can read the value of iArea. Because the value of iArea was never set to any value, iArea is equal to the default value that Java assigned to iArea when iArea was declared. When an integer is created, Java assigns the value 0 to the variable unless you tell it to do otherwise.

Click to calculate   Now we'll type code that will cause the CaluclateRectangleArea() to be executed. Let's add the code of the mouseDown() method to the MyApplet.java file. Inside the MyApplet.java file, add the following method to the MyApplet class:

```
public boolean mouseDown(java.awt.Event evt,
                         int x,
                         int y)
{

   int SideA;
   int SideB;

   SideA = 2;
   SideB = 3;

   iArea = CalculateRectangleArea(SideA, SideB);

   repaint();

   return true;

}// end of mouseDown()
```

We will discuss this method in greater detail later. For now, just note that the code inside the mouseDown() method is automatically executed whenever the user clicks the mouse inside the applet's area.

Here's how this code works. The code inside the mouseDown() method declares two integers:

```
int SideA;
int SideB;
```

Because you declared SideA and SideB inside the mouseDown() method, these variables can only be used from inside the mouseDown() method. As you might have guessed, SideA represents one side of the rectangle, and SideB represents the other side.

You then set the values of the SideA and SideB variables to 2 and 3, respectively:

```
SideA = 2;
SideB = 3;
```

Then you executed the CalculateRectangleArea() method as follows:

```
iArea = CalculateRectangleArea(SideA, SideB);
```

Recall that you declared CalculateRectangleArea() as a method that takes two parameters, both of which must be integers. Indeed, in the preceding statement you supplied two integers, SideA and SideB, as the parameters of the CalculateRectangleArea() method.

Because currently SideA is equal to 2 and SideB is equal to 3, the statement that you typed to calculate the rectangle area has an effect identical to the following statement:

```
iArea = CalculateRectangleArea(2, 3);
```

Assigning the returned value of CalculateRectangleArea() You designed the CalculateRectangleArea() method to return an integer. So when you execute the CalculateRectangleArea() method, you assigned the returned value of CalculateRectangleArea() to iArea as follows:

```
iArea = CalculateRectangleArea(SideA, SideB);
```

If currently SideA is equal to 2 and SideB is equal to 3, the CalculateRectangleArea() will return 2*3=6. So this statement has an identical effect to the following statement:

```
iArea = 6;
```

If the user clicks within the applet's area, iArea will be set to 6, the area of the rectangle. The next statement that is typed inside the mouseDown() method will then cause the paint() method to be executed:

```
repaint();
```

Java automatically executes the paint() method whenever it discovers that there is a need to repaint the applet, such as when you minimize and then maximize the window of the applet. In this example, you typed the repaint() statement because you wanted to force Java to repaint the window.

The last statement that you typed inside the mouseDown() was

```
return true;
```

Take a look at the first line of the mouseDown() method, and compare it with the first line of the CalculateRectangleArea() method. In the CalculateRectangleArea() method you have *int* as the returned value, so the CalculateRectangleArea() method must return an integer. Similarly, the mouseDown() method must return a boolean value. Java dictates what the returned value of mouseDown() should be as well as what its parameters are. (The mouse-Down() method will be discussed further later in this book.)

A *boolean* variable is a variable that can be either true or false. For example, if you declared the variable *Answer* to be of the type boolean, your declaration code would read as follows:

```
boolean Answer;
```

Then your code could set the value of Answer to be "true" as follows:

```
Answer = true;
```

Your code can also set the value of Answer to be false:

```
Answer = false;
```

But these are the only two values that can be assigned to Answer.

In the case of the mouseDown() method in this example, you returned the value true. As it turns out, in the MyApplet applet it does not matter whether you return true or false. Nevertheless, you must return a value (true or false).

Save the modified MyApplet.java file, then use JavaC.exe to compile the MyApplet.java file and to create the MyApplet.class file. Use AppletViewer to execute the MyApplet.html file. The window shown in Figure 4.4 appears.

Now click inside the applet's area; the window shown in Figure 4.5 appears.

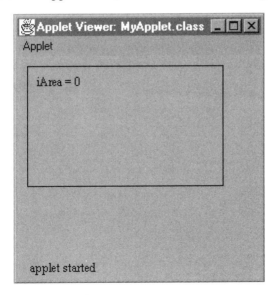

Figure 4.4: The MyApplet applet reports that the area of the rectangle is equal to 0.

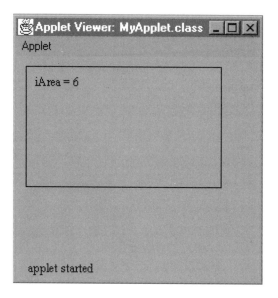

Figure 4.5: The MyApplet applet reports that the area of the rectangle is equal to 6.

THE *IF* CONDITIONAL STATEMENT

Very often, your programs will have to use conditional statements to examine values of variables. You'll now learn how to use the *if* statement in Java.

Suppose that you want to display different messages when the area of the rectangle exceeds a certain value. Modify the paint() method so that it will look like this:

```
public void paint(Graphics g)
  {

  g.drawRect(10,
            10,
            200,
            120);

  // g.drawString("Hello, I was drawn with drawString()",
  //             20,
  //             30);

  g.drawString("iArea = " + iArea,
              20,
              30);
```

```
if ( iArea == 6 )
    {
    g.drawString("B i n g o",
                 20,
                 40);
    }


if ( iArea != 6 )
    {
    g.drawString("Not a Bingo",
                 20,
                 50);
    }


if ( iArea > 6 )
    {
    g.drawString("A large rectangle",
                 20,
                 60);
    }

if ( iArea < 6 )
    {
    g.drawString("A small rectangle",
                 20,
                 70);
    }


} // end of paint()
```

The code that you added to the paint() method uses a series of *if* statements to examine the value of iArea and, depending on the outcome of the examination, the code under the *if* statement is either skipped or executed.

The first *if* statement checks to see if iArea is equal to 6:

```
if ( iArea == 6 )
    {
    g.drawString("B i n g o",
                 20,
                 40);
    }
```

Note the double equal signs (==) inside the parentheses of the *if* statement. If iArea is equal to 6, the string *B i n g o* is displayed. If iArea is not equal to 6, the code under the *if* statement is not executed.

The next *if* statement checks to see if iArea is not equal to 6:

```
if ( iArea != 6 )
    {
    g.drawString("Not a Bingo",
                20,
                50);
    }
```

Note that != represents "not equal". So if iArea is not equal to 6, the string *Not a bingo* will be displayed.

The next *if* statement checks to see if iArea is greater than 6:

```
if ( iArea > 6 )
    {
    g.drawString("A large rectangle",
                20,
                60);
    }
```

And the next *if* statement checks to see if iArea is less than 6:

```
if ( iArea < 6 )
    {
    g.drawString("A small rectangle",
                20,
                70);
    }
```

Save the modified MyApplet.java file, and then use JavaC.exe to compile the file. Use AppletViewer to view the MyApplet.html file.

The window shown in Figure 4.6 is now displayed. As shown, iArea is equal to 0 because you did not yet click the mouse inside the applet's area. Only the appropriate *if* statements were satisfied, and their corresponding strings are displayed as shown in Figure 4.6.

Click the mouse inside the applet's area, and the window shown in Figure 4.7 appears. As shown, iArea is equal to 6 because you clicked the mouse inside the applet's area. As such, only the appropriate *if* statements were satisfied, and their corresponding strings are displayed, as shown in Figure 4.7. Now terminate the MyApplet applet.

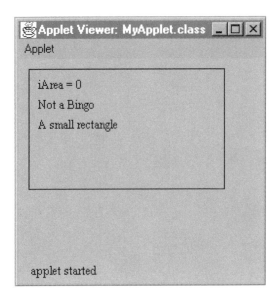

Figure 4.6: No, it ain't a bingo.

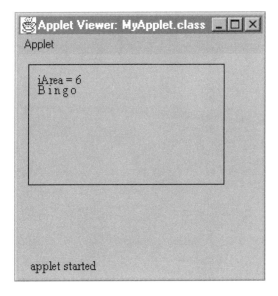

Figure 4.7: Yes, it's a bingo, all right.

THE *IF...ELSE* CONDITIONAL STATEMENT

Theoretically, the *if* statement is sufficient for examining any condition that you would like to examine. However, as is the case with all programming languages, some additional conditional statements are provided within the Java programming language.

Add the following code to the paint() method:

```
if ( iArea < 6 )
   {
   g.drawString("A small rectangle",
                20,
                80);
   }
else
   {
   g.drawString("A large rectangle",
                20,
                80);
   }
```

This code uses an *if...else* statement. If iArea is less than 6, the code under the *if* statement is executed, and the code under the *else* is not executed. If iArea is not less than 6, (for example, if iArea is equal to 6 or 7), then the code under the else statement is executed.

LOOPS

Another building block that every programming language needs is the loop mechanism. In the following example you'll implement the MyLoop applet, which demonstrates how you can use loops in Java.

1 Create the C:\Java\MyDemo\MyLoop directory. You'll save the files created for this example in this directory.

2 Use your text editor to create the MyLoop.html file, and save the file as a regular text file inside the C:\Java\MyDemo\MyLoop directory. Type the following code inside the MyLoop.html file:

```
<html>

<title>MyLoop.html</title>

<body>

<h1>This is the MyLoop.html page.</h1>
```

```
<applet code=MyLoop.class width=150 height=150>
</applet>

<hr>

This HTML page uses the MyLoop.class applet.

<hr>

</body>
</html>
```

3 Use your text editor to create the MyLoop.java file, and save the file as a regular text file inside the C:\Java\MyDemo\MyLoop directory. Type the following code inside the MyLoop.java file:

```
// MyLoop.java


import java.applet.*;
import java.awt.*;
import java.awt.peer.*;
import java.awt.image.*;
import java.io.*;
import java.net.*;
import java.util.*;

public class MyLoop extends Applet
{

int iCounter;

    public void init()
    {

    resize (250,200);

    }// end of init()


  public void paint(Graphics g)
  {

  g.drawString("Counter:" + iCounter,
            20,
            30);
```

```
g.drawRect (10,
            10,
            100,
            100);



} // end of paint()


public boolean mouseDown(java.awt.Event evt,
                         int x,
                         int y)
{

for (iCounter=0; iCounter<100; iCounter++)
    {
    repaint();
    }

return true;

}// end of mouseDown()

} // End of the class
```

4 Use JavaC.exe to compile the MyLoop.java file and to create the MyLoop.class file. Then use AppletViewer to execute the MyLoop.html file.

5 The MyLoop.class displays the text *Counter: 0.*

6 Click inside the applet's area: The MyLoop.class displays the text *Counter: 100.*

7 Select Close from the Applet menu to terminate the applet.

The for() loop The code

```
int iCounter;
```

defines the *iCounter* variable at the beginning of the class declaration. Accordingly, iCounter will be accessible by any method of the MyLoop class.

Inside the paint() method, you displayed the value of iCounter:

```
g.drawString("Counter:" + iCounter,
             20,
             30);
```

Because iCounter is equal to 0, when you start the applet the paint() method displays the text *Counter: 0.* When you click the mouse inside the applet's area, the mouseDown() method is executed:

```
public boolean mouseDown(java.awt.Event evt,
                         int x,
                         int y)
   {

   for (iCounter=0; iCounter<100; iCounter++)
      {
      repaint();
      }

   return true;

   }// end of mouseDown()

} // End of the class
```

Inside the mouseDown() method, you executed a *for()* loop:

```
for (iCounter=0; iCounter<100; iCounter++)
      {
      repaint();
      }
```

The first line of the for() loop comprises three sections:

▸ *iCounter=0* means that the loop starts by initializing the variable iCounter to 0.

▸ *iCounter<100* is a conditional statement meaning that the for() loop is executed for as long as iCounter is less than 100.

▸ iCounter++; is the same as iCounter = iCounter + 1;.

Putting it all together, the for() loop works in the following progression:

1 iCounter is set to 0.

2 iCounter is compared with 100. If iCounter is less than 100, the body of the for() loop is executed. As a result, the repaint() method is also automatically executed.

3 iCounter is increased by 1: 0+1=1. Because 1 is still less than 100, the body of the for() loop is executed again. Now the repaint() method is executed for the second time.

4 iCounter is increased by 1 to 1+1=2. Then iCounter is compared with 100, and because 2 is still less than 1, the body of the for() loop is again executed.

5 This process continues until iCounter is equal to 100, at which point the for() loop is terminated.

6 When the for() loop is finally terminated, the text *Counter: 100* is displayed on the screen.

The while() loop   With the for() loop you can create all possible loops that you can think of. However, Java also offers alternative ways to implement loops. One example is the while():

```
iCounter = 0;
while (iCounter < 100)
        {
        iCounter = iCounter  + 1;
        repaint();
        }
```

This code sets the value of iCounter to 0, and then starts a while() loop. The condition of the while() loop is

```
iCounter < 100
```

As long as iCounter is less than 100, the body of the while() loop is executed. The body of the while() loop increases the value of iCounter by 1, and then the condition of the while() loop is checked. If iCounter is still less than 100, the body of the while() loop is executed again.

In essence, the while() loop serves the same purpose as the for() loop. However, when using the for() loop, the first line of the for() loop contains the initialization (first section), the conditional statement (second section), and the increment statement (third section). Only the conditional statement is included within the while() loop; the initialization is typed before the while() loop starts, and the increment statement is typed inside the body of the while() loop.

Part 3

Java Examples

Sound with Java

The ability to play sound is a very desirable feature in modern computing. In this chapter you'll learn how to play sound from within your Java programs. This means that you'll be able to enhance your HTML pages to play sound. During the course of this chapter you'll also learn other important Java programming topics related to playing sound files, such as how to detect mouse clicking and how to make your page execute code whenever the mouse is clicked.

About sound files

You use a sound card and a microphone to record sound, and it can then be saved as a sound file. There are various sound file formats. One of the most popular is the WAV file, which has the extension .wav. However, currently Java does not support WAV sound files. Instead, Java lets you play AU files, which have the extension .au, as long as they were recorded in 8-bit mono, u-law, 8,000 Hz.

Even if future versions of Java do let you play higher-quality AU sound files (for example, a 16-bit stereo recording with a higher sampling rate), this might not be advantageous. Why? Because Java applications are oriented toward Internet applications. This means that the users of your Java application have to download the file over the Internet. A better-quality sound file means a larger sound file, which means that your user will have to spend more time downloading your application.

If you have some fantastic WAV files that you want to play in your Java applications, you'll first have to convert them to AU files. There are many utilities that can accomplish this task. For example, the Library section of the Creative Lab forum in CompuServe has a utility that converts WAV files to AU files. Other sound file conversion utilities are available over the Internet.

In the following sections you'll implement a Java applet that lets your user play AU sound files.

PREPARING THE AU SOUND FILES

In Chapter 4, you created the directory C:\Java\MyDemo. The applet you'll create in this chapter will be saved to the C:\Java\MyDemo\MySound directory, so first create this new subdirectory.

The Java software comes with a variety of sample applets. Some of these applets include sound, so let's use the AU sound files of the Java examples for the sound applet that you'll create in this chapter.

Copy the *.AU sound files from the C:\Java\Demo\BouncingHeads\Audio directory to the C:\Java\MyDemo\MySound directory. Now you have some sound AU files to practice with.

PREPARING THE HTML FILE

Now you'll create the MySound.html file, which you'll use to experiment with Java's sound playback feature.

Create a new text file with your text editor, then save it as MySound.html inside the C:\Java\MyDemo\MySound directory. Type the following code inside the MySound.html file:

```
<html>
<title>MySound.html</title>
<body>

<h1>This is the MySound.html page.</h1>

<applet code=MySound.class width=150 height=150>
</applet>

<hr>

This HTML page uses the MySound.class applet.

<hr>

</body>
</html>
```

As you can see, the MySound.html file utilizes the MySound.class applet,

```
<applet code=MySound.class width=150 height=150>
</applet>
```

which you'll implement later in the chapter.

PREPARING THE JAVA FILE

You'll now create the MySound.java file, which is the source code of the MySound.class applet.

Create a new document in your text editor and save it as MySound.java inside the C:\Java\MyDemo\MySound directory. Type the following code inside the document:

```
// MySound.java

import java.applet.*;
import java.awt.*;
import java.awt.peer.*;
import java.awt.image.*;
import java.io.*;
import java.net.*;
import java.util.*;

public class MySound extends Applet
{

  public void paint(Graphics g)
  {

  g.drawRect(10,
             10,
             120,
             120);

  play(getCodeBase(), "bong.au");

  } // end of paint()


} // End of the MySound class
```

Execute a DOS shell, make sure that you have a path to the C:\Java\Bin directory, and then at the DOS prompt type

```
JavaC MySound.java
```

Then press Enter. The JavaC.exe compiler responds by creating the MySound.class file.

At the DOS prompt, type

```
AppletViewer MySound.html
```

Then press Enter. The AppletViewer responds by displaying the window shown in Figure 5.1. If you have a sound card, you will hear the bong.au sound file.

Figure 5.1: The MyAudio.class applet executed with the AppletViewer

SEEING AND HEARING THE PAINT() METHOD

As you'll see, the code of the MyAudio.class applet was written inside the paint() method. Two things happen whenever the paint() method is executed:

- ▶ A rectangle is drawn inside the applet's area.

- ▶ The bong.au sound file is played.

You can tell that the paint() method is automatically executed when the applet is executed, because you hear the bong.au sound file when you start the MySound applet. Experiment with the MySound applet to discover other occasions when the bong.au file is played. For example, cover the applet's window with a window of another application. Then remove the other window to expose the MySound applet window. As you can hear, the bong.au sound file is played, which means that the paint() method was executed. This is no surprise, because when you expose the applet's window, Java notices and executes the paint() method because there is a need to redraw the applet's window. Also experiment by maximizing, minimizing, and restoring the applet's window.

If you drag the applet's window on the screen for a tiny distance, you will not hear the bong.au file played. Why? Because when you just slightly drag the applet's window, the operating system is responsible for displaying the window in its new location on the screen. In other words, the operating system did not notify Java that there is a need to redraw the applet's window, so Java does not execute the paint() method.

Java code for playing the sound

The entire code of the applet is inside the paint() method. As you saw in Figure 5.1, the applet has a rectangle drawn in it. The rectangle is drawn inside the paint() method:

```
g.drawRect(10,
           10,
           120,
           120);
```

The reason for drawing a rectangle is so that you can visually see that the paint() method was executed. If for some reason you don't hear the bong.au sound file—if your system does not have the capability to play AU sound files, for example, or if your sound card was not installed properly—at least you see the rectangle, and this verifies that the paint() method was executed.

Notice that your code did not directly execute the paint() method. It is the responsibility of Java to cause the automatic execution of the paint() method. This way of programming, where "somebody else" is responsible for the execution of methods, is called *event-based-programming*. Many languages use event-based programming (Visual Basic, Visual C++, Visual dBASE, and Delphi, for example). You've already seen an example: the need-to-repaint event that causes the execution of the paint() method. Another example of such an event is mouse-clicking: When the user clicks the mouse, an event occurs, and this causes another method to be executed automatically.

The last statement inside the paint() method is

```
play(getCodeBase(), "bong.au");
```

The play() method causes the sound card to play the AU sound file mentioned in the first and second parameters of the method. You supplied getCodeBase() as the first parameter of the play() method. The getCodeBase() method is very useful, as it returns the URL of the applet. No matter what directory the applet file resides in, the getCodeBase() method will return its correct URL.

The second parameter of the play() method is the string that represents that name of the file to be played. You want to play the bong.au file, so you supplied "bong.au" as the second parameter. So the bong.au file is assumed to reside in the same directory as the applet file.

Now you'll learn how to play a sound file that resides in a different directory from the applet file. Your MySound.class applet file resides inside the C:\Java\MyDemo\MySound directory. The bong.au file also resides inside this directory. You can experiment with the play() method as follows:

1 Create the C:\Java\MyDemo\MySound\Audio directory.

2 Copy the dah.au sound file from the C:\Java\MyDemo\MySound directory to your C:\Java\MyDemo\MySound\Audio directory.

3 To make sure that the experiment that you are about to perform is working as expected, delete the dah.au file from the C:\Java\MyDemo\MySound directory. Now the only place the dah.au file exists is inside the C:\Java\MyDemo\MySound\Audio directory.

4 Modify the paint() method inside the MySound.java file so that it looks like this:

```
public void paint(Graphics g)
  {

  g.drawRect(10,
             10,
             120,
             120);

  // play(getCodeBase(), "bong.au");
  play(getCodeBase(), "audio/dah.au");

  } // end of paint()
```

In this code you commented out the original play() method, and typed a new play() statement:

```
play(getCodeBase(), "audio/dah.au");
```

Now the applet will play the sound file dah.au that resides inside a directory called audio that is under the directory where the applet's files reside.

Compile the modified MySound.java file, and then execute the Applet-Viewer program to see the applet in action. Experiment with the MySound applet and then terminate it.

EXAMPLE 1: CLICK AND PLAY (CLICKNPLAY)

The ClickNPlay.class applet plays a sound file whenever the user clicks the mouse. In this example you'll create this applet and then write code that causes the applet to play the Bubble1.au sound file whenever the mouse is clicked.

1 Create a directory called C:\MyDemo\ClickNPlay.

2 Create a new text file in your text editor and call it ClickNPlay.html. Save the file into the C:\MyDemo\ClickNPlay directory. Type inside the Click-NPlay.html file the following text:

```
<html>

<title>ClickNPlay.html</title>

<body>

<h1>This is the ClickNPlay.html page.</h1>

<applet code=ClickNPlay.class width=150 height=150>
</applet>

<hr>

This HTML page uses the ClickNPlay.class applet.

<hr>

</body>
</html>
```

3 Copy the C:\MyDemo\MySound\Bubble1.au sound file to the C:\My-Demo\ClickNPlay directory, because the ClickNPlay applet plays the Bubble1.au sound file.

4 Use your text editor program to create a text file, and save the text file as ClickNPlay.java inside the C:\Java\MyDemo\ClickNPlay directory. Type the following code inside this document:

```
// ClickNPlay.java

import java.applet.*;
import java.awt.*;
import java.awt.peer.*;
import java.awt.image.*;
import java.io.*;
import java.net.*;
import java.util.*;

public class ClickNPlay extends Applet
{

  public void paint(Graphics g)
  {

  g.drawRect(10,
             10,
             120,
             120);

  } // end of paint()

    public boolean mouseDown(java.awt.Event evt,
                             int x,
                             int y)
    {

    play(getCodeBase(), "bubble1.au");
return true;

    } // End of the mouseDown() method

} // End of the ClickNPlay class
```

5 Execute a DOS shell program, and make sure that you have a path to the C:\Java\Bin directory. Use JavaC.exe to compile the ClickNPlay applet by typing the following at the DOS prompt:

```
JavaC ClickNPlay.java
```

Then press Enter.

6 Execute the ClickNPlay applet by executing the AppletViewer as follows:

```
AppletViewer ClickNPlay.html
```

Then press Enter.

7 Experiment with the ClickNPlay applet by clicking it. Every time you click the applet, the Bubble1.au file is played.

USING THE MOUSEDOWN() METHOD WITH CLICKNPLAY

The code in the above example uses the mouseDown() method:

```
public boolean mouseDown(java.awt.Event evt,
                         int x,
                         int y)
  {

  play(getCodeBase(), "bubble1.au");
  return true;

  }
```

The mouseDown() method is automatically executed whenever the user clicks the mouse on the applet's area. Note that the mouseDown() method returns a value. In particular, it returns a value that is Boolean. A Boolean variable can have one of two values: true or false. So you must use the return statement and return true or false.

When the user clicks the applet, the mouseDown() method is automatically executed. The statement that you typed inside the mouseDown() method— play(getCodeBase(), "bubble1.au");—plays the bubble1.au sound file.

THE PARAMETERS OF THE MOUSEDOWN() METHOD

The mouseDown() method has three parameters:

```
public boolean mouseDown(Event evt,
                         int x,
                         int y)
{

...
...
...

}
```

Your code did not make use of the parameters of the mouseDown() method. Nevertheless, in your future Java projects, you may find that the parameters of the mouseDown() method are useful. The *evt* parameter is used in connection with list of events. That is, when a list of events exists, the evt parameter indicates the next event in the list. (Assuming that the "mouse-is-down" event is the current event in the list, *evt* represents the next event in the list of events that are waiting to be executed.)

The x and y parameters of the mouseDown() method are integers that represent the current coordinates of the mouse cursor. These parameters are very useful, because your program can tell the exact location of the mouse cursor at the time the mouse was clicked. The next example demonstrates how this is accomplished.

EXAMPLE 2: THE WHEREAMI APPLET

In this example you'll write the WhereAmI applet, an applet that displays the coordinates of the mouse when the user clicks the mouse:

1 Create the C:\Java\MyDemo\WhereAmI directory.

2 Use your text editor to create the text file WhereAmI.html, and save the file inside the C:\Java\MyDemo\WhereAmI directory. Type the following code inside the WhereAmI.html file:

```
<html>
<title>WhereAmI.html</title>
<body>

<h1>This is the WhereAmI.html page.</h1>

<applet code=WhereAmI.class width=150 height=150>
</applet>

<hr>

This HTML page uses the WhereAmI.class applet.

<hr>

</body>
</html>
```

3 Use your text editor to create the text file WhereAmI.java, and save the file inside the C:\Java\MyDemo\WhereAmI directory. Type the following code inside the WhereAmI.java file:

```
// WhereAmI.java

import java.applet.*;
import java.awt.*;
import java.awt.peer.*;
import java.awt.image.*;
import java.io.*;
import java.net.*;
import java.util.*;

public class WhereAmI extends Applet
{

int XMousePos;
int YMousePos;

    public void paint(Graphics g)
    {
    String sXMousePos;
    String sYMousePos;

    g.drawRect(10,
               10,
               120,
               120);

    sXMousePos="Mouse X: ";
    sYMousePos="Mouse Y: ";

    sXMousePos = sXMousePos + String.valueOf(XMousePos);
    sYMousePos = sYMousePos + String.valueOf(YMousePos);


    g.drawString(sXMousePos,  25,  50);
    g.drawString(sYMousePos,  25, 100);

    } // End of paint()

        public boolean mouseDown(java.awt.Event evt,
                                 int x,
                                 int y)
        {
```

```
XMousePos = x;
YMousePos = y;

play(getCodeBase(), "ooh.au");

repaint();

return true;

} // End of mouseDown()

} // End of the WhereAmI class
```

4 Execute a DOS shell program, make sure that you have a path to the C:\Java\Bin directory, log into the C:\Java\MyDemo\WhereAmI directory, and compile the WhereAmI.java file by typing the following at the DOS prompt:

```
JavaC WhereAmI.java
```

Then press Enter. JavaC.exe responds by compiling the WhereAmI.java file, and the WhereAmI.class file is created.

5 At the DOS prompt type

```
AppletViewer WhereAmI.html
```

Then press Enter. AppletViewer responds by displaying the window shown in Figure 5.2.

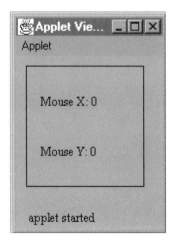

Figure 5.2: The AppletViewer executing the WhereAmI applet

6 Click at various places inside the applet, and verify that the program displays the coordinates of the mouse. Then terminate the applet.

DECLARING VARIABLES THAT ARE ACCESSIBLE TO EVERY METHOD

At the beginning of the WhereAmI class you declared two variables:

```
public class WhereAmI extends Applet
{

int XMousePos;
int YMousePos;

...
... Methods of the class
...

} // End of the WhereAmI class
```

XMousePos is declared as an integer variable, and YMousePos is also declared as an integer. The XMousePos is a variable that will hold the x coordinate of the mouse, and the YMousePos variable will hold the y coordinate of the mouse.

It is important to note that the XMousePos and YMousePos were not declared inside any method of the WhereAmI class. This means that any method can access these variables.

THE MOUSEDOWN() METHOD OF THE WHEREAMI CLASS

Inside the mouseDown() method of the WhereAmI class you set the values of the variables XMousePos and YMousePos as follows:

```
public boolean mouseDown(java.awt.Event evt,
                         int x,
                         int y)
   {

   XMousePos = x;
   YMousePos = y;

   ...
   ...
   ...

   } // End of the mouseDown() method
```

Again, x and y are parameters of the mouseDown() method, and these parameters represent the mouse coordinates at the time it is clicked. If you try to use the x and y variables outside the mouseDown() method, you'll get a compiling error. Why? Because only the mouseDown() method can access the x and y variables. No other methods inside the WhereAmI class know about the x and y variables.

You set the values of XMousePos and YMousePos as follows:

```
XMousePos = x;
YMousePos = y;
```

XMousePos and YMousePos still represent the *x* and *y* coordinates of the mouse at the time of the clicking. However, because XMousePos and YMousePos were declared at the beginning of the WhereAmI class, the mouse coordinates are now known inside *any* method of the WhereAmI class. That is, if another method needs to know the mouse coordinates at the time of the clicking, that method can access the XMousePos and YMousePos variables.

> **Note:** You just learned that the XMousePos variable is accessible from any method of the class. In programming terminology, this means that the scope of the XMousePos variable is throughout the entire WhereAmI class. On the other hand, the scope of the x integer of the mouseDown() method is inside the mouseDown() method.

REPAINTING THE APPLET AREA

The next statement that you typed inside the mouseDown() method of the WhereAmI class plays the ooh.au sound file:

```
play(getCodeBase(), "ooh.au");
```

Every time the user clicks the mouse, the ooh.au sound file will be played.

Then you executed the following statement:

```
repaint();
```

The repaint() method causes the execution of the paint() method. Recall that the paint() method is automatically executed whenever Java decides that it is necessary to repaint the applet's area. But there are occasions where you want to force the execution of the paint() method. For example, once the user clicks the mouse, Java does not find it necessary to repaint the applet's area. But in this example, you want to repaint the applet's area because you want to display the new coordinates of the mouse. The way to force the execution of the paint() method is by executing the repaint() method.

The last statement that you typed inside the mouseDown() method is

```
return true;
```

Again, the only reason you return a value from the mouseDown() method is because the mouseDown() method must return false or true.

DISPLAYING THE MOUSE COORDINATES

The code that displays the mouse coordinates is inside the paint() method.

You declared two strings inside the paint() method:

```
public void paint(Graphics g)
  {
  String sXMousePos;
  String sYMousePos;



  ...
  ...
  ...


  } // End of the paint() method
```

sXMousePos and sYMousePos are variables that can hold strings. You declared sXMousePos and sYMousePos inside the paint() method. This means that only the paint() method has access to these variables. Why didn't you declare the sXMousePos and sYMousePos at the beginning if the WhereAmI class? Because, as it turns out, only the paint() method needs to access these variables.

The drawRect() method is executed to draw a rectangle inside the applet's area:

```
g.drawRect(10,
           10,
           120,
           120);
```

Dealing with strings The next two statements assign values to the string variables:

```
sXMousePos="Mouse X: ";
  sYMousePos="Mouse Y: ";
```

At this point in the program, the sXMousePos variable is equal to Mouse X:, and the sYMousePos string is equal to Mouse Y:.

Then, the sXMousePos and sYMousePos strings are set as follows:

```
sXMousePos = sXMousePos + String.valueOf(XMousePos);
  sYMousePos = sYMousePos + String.valueOf(YMousePos);
```

Let's take a look at what is happening to the sXMousePos string. Previously, the sXMousePos string was set to Mouse X:. The preceding statement sets the sXMousePos string as follows:

```
sXMousePos = sXMousePos + String.valueOf(XMousePos);
```

So now sXMousePos is equal to its previous value, plus another value. The other value that was added to sXMousePos is

```
String.valueOf(XMousePos)
```

Recall that once the user clicks the mouse, XMousePos is updated with the X coordinates of the mouse. The XMousePos variable is an integer. It can be used inside paint() because this variable is accessible by every method of the WhereAmI class. So if at the time of the clicking the mouse cursor was 15 pixels from the left edge of the applet's area, XMousePos is equal to 15. If you type the following statement:

```
sXMousePos = sXMousePos + String.valueOf(XMousePos);;
```

Java will convert the integer 15 to the string "15", and sXMousePos will be equal to Mouse X: 15.

You can convert an integer to a string as follows:

```
String.valueOf(XMousePos)
```

The parameter of the valueOf() method is the value of the integer that you are trying to convert to a string. Also, note that a period separates the word *String* from the *valueOf()* method.

Displaying text   The last statement that you typed inside the paint() method uses the drawString() method to display the values of the sXMousePos string and the value of the sYMousePos string:

```
g.drawString(sXMousePos,  25,  50);
g.drawString(sYMousePos,  25, 100);
```

These two statements display the values of the strings. sXMousePos is displayed 25 pixels from the left edge of the applet and 50 pixels from the top edge of the applet. The sYMousePos string is displayed 25 pixels from the left edge of the applet and 100 pixels from the top edge of the applet.

CONVENTIONS: VARIABLE NAMES AND METHOD NAMES

In the previous example, you set the name of the integer to XMousePos and the name of the string to sXMousePos. The *s* indicates that the sXMousePos variable was declared as string. This is *not* a Java requirement. However, when writing programs it is better to adopt some type of naming convention; this way your program will be easier to read and understand. For example, the integer XMousePos could have been called iXMousePos, where the *i* is a hint that this variable is an integer.

Note that XMousePos and YMousePos are accessible from any method inside the WhereAmI class. Some programmers like to think of these variables as global variables, and they precede the names of these variables with the *g* character, as in gXMousePos and gYMousePos. This way, whenever you see a variable that starts with the letter *g*, you know that the variable was declared at the beginning of the class and is accessible from any method. However, you may decide that a better name for the XMousePos position is giXMousePos, where now it is clear that the variable is global as well as an integer.

And what about methods? You saw that Java uses "internal" method names, such as mouseDown(), paint(), and repaint(). In other words, Java starts the names of methods with a lowercase character. When the program is very large and contains hundreds of methods, some of these methods will be executed automatically by Java (such as paint() and mouseDown()), and some will be methods that you are responsible for executing (such as Calculate()). If you name your own methods with names that start with a lowercase character, you may in the future forget whether the method is a Java method or a method that was completely written by you. You can solve this name convention problem by using various tricks. You may decide that every method written by you should begin with the characters *ab*—for example, ab_Calculate(). Alternatively, you may make the convention rule that every method that you write by yourself will start with an uppercase character, such as Calculate(). Again, these are not Java requirements, but when your Java programs have thousands of lines of code, you'll be sorry if you did not adopt a consistent name convention for variables and methods.

One last word of advice about name conventions: Do not use variable names and method names that are all capital letters. For example, do not use XMOUSE-POS as the name of a variable or CALCULATE() as the name of a method. In programming, uppercase names are typically used to denote constants. For example, if your code repeatedly uses the number 1.23456789, you may declare at the beginning of the class a constant called STRANGENUMBER that represents the number 1.23456789. Then whenever your code needs to use the number 1.23456789, you can substitute the term *STRANGENUMBER*.

Graphics and
Images

6

Displaying graphics and images is a very popular feature in Web publishing. In this chapter you'll learn how to display graphics and images from within your Java applets. This means that you'll be able to enhance your HTML pages to display impressive images and graphics. Furthermore, your users will also be able to draw graphics by using a mouse.

ABOUT GIF FILES

There are many formats for saving graphics files, including BMP, PCX, PICT, JPEG, and GIF. Java lets you display images that were saved as GIF files, one of the most popular formats in use on the Internet.

> **Note:** There are many programs that enable you to handle GIF files. Surf the Internet or forums on online services like CompuServe, Prodigy, or America Online to find a shareware program that lets you convert files saved in other formats to GIF files.

TRANSPARENT GIF FILES

Figure 6.1 shows three GIF files that are displayed using the WinGif program. The top window of Figure 6.1 shows the C:\Java\Demo\Animator\Images\ Duke\T1.GIF image; the middle window shows the T2.GIF picture; and the bottom window shows the T3.GIF picture. During the course of this chapter and the next chapter, you'll experiment with these GIF files, which come with Java and reside in the C:\Java\Demo\Animator\Images\Duke directory.

Figure 6.1: GIF pictures displayed with WinGif

In Figure 6.1, T1.GIF, T2.GIF, and T3.GIF have gray backgrounds. What will happen when you display these images inside the window of an applet? Let's say that the background of the applet is red. Will the pictures be displayed as shown in Figure 6.2, where the image has changed to match the background color of the applet? Or will the files be displayed with their original background, no matter what the background of the applet is, as in Figure 6.3? We will answer these questions during the course of this chapter.

There are many programs that enable you to generate transparent GIF files. When the image of a transparent GIF file is placed inside a window, the background of the image changes to match the background of the window. Here's how you make one:

1 Save your picture as a GIF file using a program like WinGif.

2 Use a utility that converts the GIF file to a transparent GIF file (one such utility is GIFTRANS.EXE).

Note: Surf the Internet or online-service forums to find a program that lets you convert a GIF file to a transparent GIF file, such as GIFTRANS.EXE for DOS.

Figure 6.2: The background color of the image has changed to match the background color of the applet.

Figure 6.3: The background color of the image was not changed to match the background color of the applet.

3 Let's say that you have a GIF picture file called MyNonTrans.GIF. You now have to decide what color to use for the background of MyNon-Trans.GIF. The color that you'll use for the background of the MyNon-Trans.GIF file must not be used for any other part of the picture. Once you decide on the color, paint the background color of MyNonTrans.GIF with it. Let's assume that you decided to paint the background of My-NonTrans.GIF with red. (You can use any paint program such as Paint-brush to paint the background of a BMP picture, and then convert the BMP file to a GIF file).

4 At this point you have a GIF file called MyNonTrans.GIF, whose back-ground color is red. You can now create the IAmTrans.GIF transparent GIF with GIFTRANS.EXE as follows:

```
giftrans -t #ff0000 MyNonTrans.gif > IAmTrans.GIF
```

Then press Enter.

In the preceding command you executed the GIFTRANS.EXE program to convert the MyNonTrans.GIF file to a new file called IAmTrans.GIF. The pa-rameter #ff0000 was used because you painted the background of MyNon-Trans.GIF red. Had you decided to paint the background green, the parameter would have been #00ff00. Had you decided to use blue, the parameter would have been #0000ff. When using white as the background color, use the #ffffff parameter. When using black as the background color, use #000000.

Again, assuming that you decided on a red background, when you place the IAmTrans.GIF file inside a window, all the red pixels of the image will be displayed with the color of the window on which it has been placed. If the transparent GIF file was placed inside a window whose background color is yellow, all the red pixels of IAmTrans.GIF will be drawn as yellow pixels.

This discussion about transparent GIF files was provided so that you'll be able to generate your own image files for your Java programs after obtaining the appropriate programs to do so. However, you'll be able to perform the examples in this chapter and the next chapter without any special software, because they utilize the GIF files that are provided with Java.

EXAMPLE 1: LETTING YOUR USER DRAW INSIDE THE APPLET

Here's how you can let your user draw graphics inside your HTML page:

1 Create the C:\Java\MyDemo\DrawIt directory.

2 Use your text editor to create the DrawIt.html file, and save it as a regular text file inside the C:\Java\MyDemo\DrawIt directory. Type the following code inside DrawIt.html:

```
<html>
<title>DrawIt.html</title>

<body>

<h1>This is the DrawIt.html page.</h1>

<applet code=DrawIt.class width=250 height=250>
</applet>

<hr>

This HTML page uses the DrawIt.class applet.

<hr>

</body>
</html>
```

3 Use your text editor program to create the DrawIt.java file, and save it as a regular text file inside the C:\Java\MyDemo\DrawIt directory. Type the following code inside the DrawIt.java file:

```
// DrawIt.java

import java.applet.*;
import java.awt.*;
import java.awt.peer.*;
import java.awt.image.*;
import java.io.*;
import java.net.*;
import java.util.*;

public class DrawIt extends Applet
{

int XMousePosOld;
int YMousePosOld;

int XMousePosNew;
int YMousePosNew;

Graphics gg;

boolean GotThegg = false;

 public void paint(Graphics g)
  {

  g.drawRect(10,
           10,
           230,
           230);


  } // end of paint()


  public boolean mouseDrag(java.awt.Event evt,
                          int x,
                          int y)
  {

  XMousePosNew = x;
  YMousePosNew = y;
```

```
if ( GotThegg == false )
   {
   gg = getGraphics();
   GotThegg = true;
   }


  gg.drawLine (XMousePosOld,
               YMousePosOld,
               XMousePosNew,
               YMousePosNew);

XMousePosOld = XMousePosNew;
YMousePosOld = YMousePosNew;


return true;

} // end of mouseDrag()


public boolean mouseDown(java.awt.Event evt,
                         int x,
                         int y)
{

XMousePosOld = x;
YMousePosOld = y;

return true;

} // end of mouseDown()



} // End of the class
```

4 Execute a DOS shell, make sure you have a path to the C:\Java\Bin directory, log into the C:\Java\MyDemo\DrawIt directory, and at the DOS prompt type

```
JavaC DrawIt.java
```

Then press Enter. The JavaC.exe compiler responds by compiling the DrawIt.java file and creating the DrawIt.class file.

5 At the DOS prompt type

```
AppletViewer DrawIt.html
```

Then press Enter. The AppletViewer program displays the DrawIt applet.

6 You can now use the mouse to draw inside the applet. For example, Figure 6.4 shows the DrawIt applet with the name *Gurewich & Gurewich* drawn in it. To draw, hold down the mouse button while moving the mouse. The DrawIt applet will draw according to the mouse's movement.

Figure 6.4: Drawing with the DrawIt applet

SAVING MOUSE COORDINATES AS GLOBAL VARIABLES

The code that you typed inside the DrawIt class starts by declaring four integer variables that are accessible by all the methods of the class:

```
public class DrawIt extends Applet
{

int XMousePosOld;
int YMousePosOld;

int XMousePosNew;
int YMousePosNew;

...
...
...
```

```
} // End of the DrawIt class.
```

Again, because the preceding four variables are declared at the beginning of the class (outside any method of the DrawIt class), these four integer variables are accessible by all the methods of the class.

You also declared the following variables at the beginning of the DrawIt class:

```
Graphics gg;

boolean GotThegg = false;
```

The purpose of these variables will be explained later in this chapter.

THE MOUSEDOWN() METHOD

The mouseDown() method is executed whenever the user presses the mouse button down. The x and y parameters of mouseDown() represent the mouse coordinates at the time the mouse button is pressed:

```
public boolean mouseDown(java.awt.Event evt,
                         int x,
                         int y)
{

...
...
...

} // end of mouseDown()
```

Inside the mouseDown() method you updated the XMousePosOld and YMousePosOld with the x and y parameters:

```
XMousePosOld = x;
YMousePosOld = y;
```

The return statement is then executed (note that the mouseDown() method must return true or false):

```
return true;
```

DRAWING A RECTANGLE INSIDE THE APPLET

Inside the paint() method, you simply drew a rectangle:

```
public void paint(Graphics g)
  {

  g.drawRect(10,
```

```
            10,
            230,
            230);
```

```
} // end of paint()
```

Note that the drawRect() method is executed on the *g* parameter of the paint() method. *g* is a variable of type Graphics that represents the applet's graphical area.

THE MOUSEDRAG() METHOD

The mouseDrag() method is automatically executed whenever the user drags the mouse. Note that the mouseDrag() method has identical parameters as the mouseDown() method:

```
public boolean mouseDrag(java.awt.Event evt,
                         int x,
                         int y)
  {

  …
  …
  …

  }
```

The statements that you typed inside the mouseDrag() method update the XMousePosNew and YMousePosNew variables as follows:

```
XMousePosNew = x;
  YMousePosNew = y;
```

At this point in the program, the XMousePosOld and YMousePosOld variables are updated with the coordinates of the mouse at the time the mouse button was first pressed down, and the XMousePosNew and YMousePosNew variables are updated with the coordinates of the mouse at the time the mouse-Drag() method is executed.

All you have to do is connect the point (XMousePosOld, YMousePosOld) with the point (XMousePosNew, YMousePosNew). You connect these two points with a straight line by using the drawLine() method:

```
gg.drawLine (XMousePosOld,
             YMousePosOld,
             XMousePosNew,
             YMousePosNew);
```

The first two parameters of the drawLine() method represent the starting point of the line, and the third and fourth parameters of the drawLine() method represent the ending point of the line.

THE GETGRAPHICS() METHOD

The important thing to note about the code inside the mouseDrag() method is that unlike the paint() method, the mouseDrag() method does not have *g* as its parameter. When a method has *g* as its parameter, it is very easy to draw inside the applet. For example, you can draw a rectangle inside the paint() method as follows:

```
g.drawRect(10,
           10,
           230,
           230);
```

Since the mouseDrag() method does not have *g* as its parameter, you'll have to extract the *g* by yourself. The good news is that extracting the *g* of the applet is very easy, thanks to the getGraphics() method. GetGraphics() returns a value that represents the graphical area of the applet. If you have to draw the line inside paint(), you can use the following statement:

```
g.drawLine (XMousePosOld,
            YMousePosOld,
            XMousePosNew,
            YMousePosNew);
```

Inside the mouseDrag() method you can use the drawLine() method by applying it on the returned value of getGraphics():

```
if ( GotThegg == false )
    {
    gg = getGraphics();
    GotThegg = true;
    }
```

Once gg is extracted, you can draw the line:

```
gg.drawLine (XMousePosOld,
             YMousePosOld,
             XMousePosNew,
             YMousePosNew);
```

An *if* statement is executed to examine the value of GotThegg. Recall that at the beginning of the DrawIt class you declared GotThegg as follows:

```
boolean GotThegg = false;
```

So when the mouseDrag() method is executed for the first time, GotThegg is equal to false, and the code under the if statement is executed. This code extracts the value of *gg*, and also sets GotThegg to true. So the next time mouseDrag() is executed, GotThegg is already equal to true, and the code under the if statement is not executed again.

Recall also that *gg* was declared at the beginning of the DrawIt class as follows:

```
Graphics gg;
```

So *gg* is a variable of type Graphics (a variable that represents a graphical area where you can draw).

Why do you want to extract *gg* only once? Because every time you extract *gg*, a memory area in the PC is allocated to *gg*. If you keep extracting gg for each execution of the mouseDrag() method, sooner or later the PC will run out of memory.

Now a line has been drawn from the point where the mouse button was pressed to the current location of the mouse cursor. The next two statements that you execute inside the mouseDrag() method are

```
XMousePosOld = XMousePosNew;
```

and

```
YMousePosOld = YMousePosNew;
```

The next time the mouseDrag() method is executed, a line will be drawn from the ending point of the previous line to the current location of the mouse cursor.

Because the mouseDrag() method must return a value of true or false, the last statement is

```
return true;
```

HOW OFTEN IS THE MOUSEDRAG() METHOD EXECUTED?

Let's say that you have a user who keeps dragging the mouse continuously. Will the mouseDrag() method be executed continuously? The answer is no. In fact, if the PC executed the mouseDrag() method continuously, it would not be able to perform other tasks.

The designers of the PC solved the problem by including special hardware circuitry that periodically checks to see whether the mouse was moved. If it has, a special memory cell is updated with the new coordinates of the mouse cursor. At regular intervals the operating system checks the memory cell that is updated with new mouse coordinates. If the mouse coordinates are different than the last mouse coordinates known to the operating system, the operating system concludes that the mouse was moved, and the mouseDrag() method is executed.

In other words, the operating system does not check the mouse's status constantly. If the mouse is moved several times between checks, the operating system may believe it was moved only once. Theoretically, the following scenario could have happened:

1 The mouse was moved from point A to B.

2 The mouse was moved from point B to C.

3 The mouse was moved from point C to D.

4 The mouse was moved from point D back to point A.

Let's say that these movements occurred very quickly, so that when the operating system checked the mouse status, it found that the mouse is back at point A. In this case, the mouseDrag() method will not be executed, and no line will be drawn at all. In other words, if you move the mouse fast enough, the applet will miss a lot of lines.

In practice, the fact that lines can be missed when the mouse is dragged very fast is rarely a problem, as long as the user moves the mouse gently.

EXAMPLE 2: DRAWING ARCS

In the same manner in which you connected points with straight lines, you can connect points with arcs. The following examples illustrate this procedure.

In this example you'll modify the DrawIt applet so that instead of connecting the points with straight lines, small arcs are drawn. This demonstrates how the drawArc() method works.

1 Modify the mouseDrag() method of the DrawIt.java applet so that it looks as follows:

```
public boolean mouseDrag(java.awt.Event evt,
                         int x,
                         int y)

   {

   XMousePosNew = x;
   YMousePosNew = y;
```

```
if ( GotThegg == false )
  {
  gg = getGraphics();
  GotThegg = true;
  }


// gg.drawLine (XMousePosOld,
//               YMousePosOld,
//               XMousePosNew,
//               YMousePosNew);


gg.drawArc(XMousePosOld,
           YMousePosOld,
           25,
           25,
           0,
           90);

XMousePosOld = XMousePosNew;
YMousePosOld = YMousePosNew;


return true;

} // end of mouseDrag()
```

In this code you commented out the drawLine() method and instead
added the drawArc() method:

```
gg.drawArc(XMousePosOld,
           YMousePosOld,
           25,
           25,
           0,
           90);
```

2 Use JavaC.exe to compile the DrawIt.java file to create the DrawIt.class
file, and then execute the AppletViewer to display the DrawIt.html applet.

3 Drag the mouse, and notice that now the DrawIt applet draws small arcs.
Figure 6.5 shows the window of the DrawIt applet after the mouse is
dragged.

Figure 6.5: The modified DrawIt applet draws small arcs as the user drags the mouse.

DRAWING ARCS WITH THE DRAWARC() METHOD

As its name implies, the drawArc() method draws arcs:

```
gg.drawArc(XMousePosOld,
        YMousePosOld,
        25,
        25,
        0,
        90);
```

The arc is a portion of a circle. The circle is enclosed by an imaginary rectangle. The coordinates of the upper-left corner of the imaginary rectangle are provided by the first and second parameters of the drawArc() method. The width and height of the imaginary rectangle are specified in the third and fourth parameters of the drawArc() method.

The first parameter of the drawArc() method specifies the starting point of the arc. *0* means that the arc starts at 0 degrees. The sixth parameter of the drawArc() method specifies the ending point of the arc. Using a positive number will cause the arc to be drawn in a counterclockwise direction. You supplied 90 as the sixth parameter of the drawArc() method. This means that the arc will be drawn in a counterclockwise direction from 0 degrees to 90 degrees (one quarter of a circle). As the user drags the mouse, the mouseDrag() method will be executed. Whenever the mouseDrag() method is executed, a quarter of a circle will be drawn at the point where the mouse cursor is located.

EXAMPLE 3: DRAWING CIRCLES

In the previous example you drew arcs. Now you'll draw complete circles.

1 Modify the mouseDrag() method inside the DrawIt.java file so that the mouseDrag() method will look as follows:

```
public boolean mouseDrag(java.awt.Event evt,
                         int x,
                         int y)
  {

XMousePosNew = x;
YMousePosNew = y;

if ( GotThegg == false )
   {
   gg = getGraphics();
   GotThegg = true;
   }


   gg.drawArc(XMousePosOld,
              YMousePosOld,
              25,
              25,
              0,
              360);

XMousePosOld = XMousePosNew;
YMousePosOld = YMousePosNew;

return true;

  } // end of mouseDrag()
```

2 Execute the JavaC.exe program to compile the DrawIt.java file and create the DrawIt.class file.

3 Execute the DrawIt.class applet with the AppletViewer program. Drag the mouse and notice that whenever the mouseDrag() method is executed, a small circle is drawn. Figure 6.6 shows the applet after the mouse is dragged.

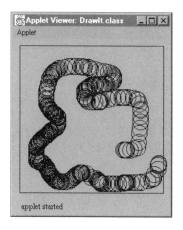

Figure 6.6: Drawing circles with the modified DrawIt applet

DRAWING CIRCLES WITH THE DRAWARC() METHOD

If you draw an arc from 0 to 360, you are drawing a complete circle. This is the reason you supplied 0 as the fifth parameter of the drawArc() method and 360 as the sixth parameter of the drawArc() method:

```
gg.drawArc(XMousePosOld,
           YMousePosOld,
           25,
           25,
           0,
           360);
```

EXAMPLE 4: FILLING GRAPHIC OBJECTS

The next example illustrates how you can draw filled (solid) arcs.

1 Modify the mouseDrag() method inside the DrawIt.java file so that it looks as follows:

```
public boolean mouseDrag(java.awt.Event evt,
                         int x,
                         int y)
  {

XMousePosNew = x;
YMousePosNew = y;
```

```
if ( GotThegg == false )
   {
   gg = getGraphics();
   GotThegg = true;
   }


  gg.fillArc(XMousePosOld,
             YMousePosOld,
             55,
             55,
             0,
             45);

XMousePosOld = XMousePosNew;
YMousePosOld = YMousePosNew;


return true;

} // end of mouseDrag()
```

2 Use the JavaC.exe compiler program to compile the DrawIt.java file for creating the DrawIt.class file.

3 Use the AppletViewer program to execute DrawIt.html. Drag the mouse, and notice that now every time the mouseDrag() method is executed an arc from 0 to 45 degrees is drawn. The arc is filled with a solid color (see Figure 6.7).

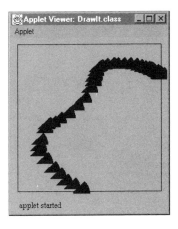

Figure 6.7: Drawing a filled (solid) arc

To draw a filled arc, you used the fillArc() method inside the mouseDrag() method:

```
gg.fillArc(XMousePosOld,
           YMousePosOld,
           55,
           55,
           0,
           45);
```

EXAMPLE 5: DRAWING FILLED (SOLID) CIRCLES

By applying the fillArc() method to draw arcs from 0 to 360 degrees, you are drawing filled circles, as illustrated in the following examples:

1 Modify the mouseDrag() method inside the DrawIt.java file so that it looks as follows:

```
public boolean mouseDrag(java.awt.Event evt,
                         int x,
                         int y)
  {

  XMousePosNew = x;
  YMousePosNew = y;

  if ( GotThegg == false )
    {
    gg = getGraphics();
    GotThegg = true;
    }

    gg.fillArc(XMousePosOld,
               YMousePosOld,
               15,
               15,
               0,
               360);

  XMousePosOld = XMousePosNew;
  YMousePosOld = YMousePosNew;


  return true;

  } // end of mouseDrag()
```

2 Use the JavaC.exe compiler to compile the DrawIt.java file to create the DrawIt.class file.

3 Use the AppletViewer program to execute DrawIt.html. Drag the mouse, and notice that a filled circle is drawn every time the mouseDrag() method is executed (see Figure 6.8).

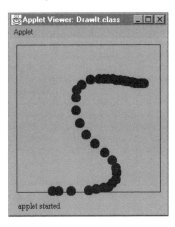

Figure 6.8: Drawing filled (solid) circles with the modified DrawIt applet

You drew the filled circles with the fillArc() method as follows:

```
gg().fillArc(XMousePosOld,
             YMousePosOld,
             15,
             15,
             0,
             360);
```

The fifth and sixth parameters of the fillArc() method instruct the fillArc() method to draw an arc from 0 to 360 degrees, a full circle.

EXAMPLE 6: DRAWING FILLED (SOLID) RECTANGLES

In the next example you'll draw a filled rectangle whenever the mouseDrag() method is executed.

1 Modify the mouseDrag() method inside the DrawIt.java file so that it looks as follows:

```
public boolean mouseDrag(java.awt.Event evt,
                         int x,
                         int y)
   {

   XMousePosNew = x;
   YMousePosNew = y;

   if ( GotThegg == false )
      {
      gg = getGraphics();
      GotThegg = true;
      }

    gg.fillRect(XMousePosOld,
                YMousePosOld,
                20,
                20);


   XMousePosOld = XMousePosNew;
   YMousePosOld = YMousePosNew;


   return true;

   } // end of mouseDrag()
```

2 Use the JavaC.exe program to compile the DrawIt.java file and create the DrawIt.class file.

3 Use the AppletViewer program to execute the DrawIt.html file. Drag the mouse, and notice that every time the mouseDrag() method is executed, a filled rectangle is drawn (see Figure 6.9).

SETTING COLORS FOR YOUR DRAWINGS

So far all the drawings you have created were drawn with the default color, black. In the following examples you'll set a different color for your drawing.

Figure 6.9: Drawing filled rectangles with the modified DrawIt applet

In this example you'll draw the filled rectangles with red.

1 Modify the mouseDrag() method inside the DrawIt.java file as follows:

```
public boolean mouseDrag(java.awt.Event evt,
                         int x,
                         int y)
   {

XMousePosNew = x;
YMousePosNew = y;

if ( GotThegg == false )
   {
   gg = getGraphics();
   GotThegg = true;
   }

   gg.setColor(Color.red);

   gg.fillRect(XMousePosOld,
               YMousePosOld,
               20,
               20);


XMousePosOld = XMousePosNew;
YMousePosOld = YMousePosNew;
```

```
    return true;

} // end of mouseDrag()
```

2 Compile the DrawIt.java file to create the DrawIt.class file, and then execute the DrawIt.class applet with the AppletViewer program.

3 Drag the mouse, and notice that now the filled rectangles are drawn with red (see Figure 6.10).

Figure 6.10: Drawing with red

THE SETCOLOR() METHOD

You can set a new color as follows:

```
gg.setColor(Color.red);
```

The setColor() method sets the color that will be used when drawing inside the gg area. The parameter that you supplied to the setColor() method is Color.red, which represents the red color.

Once you have supplied the color to the SetColor() method, apply the fillRect() method on gg:

```
gg.fillRect(XMousePosOld,
            YMousePosOld,
            5,
            5);
```

Because the current color is red, the filled rectangles are drawn in red.

EXAMPLE 7: LOADING AND DISPLAYING GIF FILES

So far, you have drawn graphics using various graphics methods, including drawLine(), drawRect(), drawArc(), fillRect(),and fillArc(). Now you'll display a GIF picture whenever the mouseDrag() method is executed.

In this example you'll load the T1.GIF picture file and then draw this picture whenever the mouse is dragged. The T1.GIF picture is shown on the top window of Figure 6.1.

1 Make sure that the T1.GIF file resides inside your C:\Java\MyDemo\ DrawIt directory. (You can copy this file from your C:\Java\Demo\Animator\Images\Duke directory.)

2 At the beginning of the DrawIt class inside the DrawIt.java file, add the declaration of the MyImage variable so that the beginning of the DrawIt class is as follows:

```
public class DrawIt extends Applet
{

int XMousePosOld;
int YMousePosOld;

int XMousePosNew;
int YMousePosNew;

Graphics gg;

boolean GotThegg = false;

Image MyImage;

...
...
...
}// end of class declaration
```

3 Modify the mouseDraw() method inside the DrawIt.java file as follows:

```
public boolean mouseDrag(java.awt.Event evt,
                         int x,
                         int y)
  {

XMousePosNew = x;
```

```
        YMousePosNew = y;

        if ( GotThegg == false )
           {
           gg = getGraphics();
           GotThegg = true;

           MyImage = getImage(getCodeBase(), "t1.gif" );

           }

           gg.drawImage(MyImage,
                        XMousePosOld,
                        YMousePosOld,
                        null);

        XMousePosOld = XMousePosNew;
        YMousePosOld = YMousePosNew;


        return true;

        } // end of mouseDrag()
```

4 Use the JavaC.exe program to create the DrawIt.class file from the DrawIt.java file, and then execute the AppletViewer program to execute DrawIt.html.

5 Drag the mouse, and notice that whenever mouseDrag() method is executed, the T1.GIF file is drawn at the coordinate where the mouse cursor is located (see Figure 6.11).

You declared the MyImage variable as follows:

```
Image MyImage;
```

This statement declares MyImage as a variable of type Image. This means that MyImage is a variable that represents a picture—in this case, a GIF file.

Assign a value to MyImage as follows:

```
MyImage = getImage(getCodeBase(), "t1.gif" );
```

In this statement you used the getImage() method to set the value of MyImage. Note that the first parameter of getImage() is getCodeBase(). Recall from Chapter 5 that the getCodeBase() method returns the name of the directory where the applet file (DrawIt.class) resides. The second parameter of getImage() method is the name of the GIF file that you are assigning to the MyImage

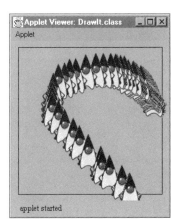

Figure 6.11: Drawing the Duke (T1.GIF) whenever the mouseDrag() method is executed

variable. It is assumed that T1.GIF resides inside the same directory as the applets. This method of setting the value of MyImage is identical to the method that you used to set the value of the AU sound file in Chapter 5.

If you want to place the GIF file in a different directory, you have to set the second parameter of getImage() accordingly. For example, you can create the C:\Java\MyDemo\DrawIt\Images directory, and place the T1.GIF file inside this directory. The statement that sets the value of MyImage would then be

```
MyImage = getImage(getCodeBase(), "Images/t1.gif" );
```

gg represents the graphical area of the applet and *MyImage* represents the T1.GIF picture. You can display T1.GIF as follows:

```
gg.drawImage(MyImage,
             XMousePosOld,
             YMousePosOld,
             null);
```

The first parameter of drawImage() is the image that you want to draw. The second and third parameters of drawImage() are the coordinates where you want to place the image. The fourth parameter of drawImage() is null. This parameter can be used in conjunction with a Java feature that lets you keep track of whether or not the image was drawn successfully. Because this feature is not used in the DrawIt applet, the fourth parameter of drawImage() is set to null.

EXAMPLE 8: SCALING THE IMAGE

In the previous example you drew the T1.GIF image in its natural (original) size. However, Java also lets you stretch the image to scale it up or down. Here's how to display a magnified image:

1 Modify the mouseDrag() method inside the DrawIt.java file to look as follows:

```
public boolean mouseDrag(java.awt.Event evt,
                         int x,
                         int y)
  {

XMousePosNew = x;
YMousePosNew = y;

if ( GotThegg = false )
   {
   gg = getGraphics();
   GotThegg = true;

   MyImage = getImage(getCodeBase(), "t1.gif" );
   }


   gg.drawImage(MyImage,
                XMousePosOld,
                YMousePosOld,
                150,
                150,
                null);

XMousePosOld = XMousePosNew;
YMousePosOld = YMousePosNew;


   return true;

} // end of mouseDrag()
```

2 Use JavaC.exe to compile the DrawIt.java file and create the DrawIt.class file. Use AppletViewer to execute DrawIt.html.

3 Drag the mouse, and notice that whenever the mouseDrag() method is executed, the T1.GIF file is drawn (see Figure 6.12). The T1.GIF picture is displayed magnified.

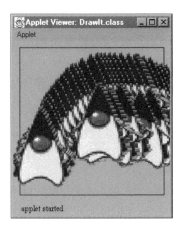

Figure 6.12: Drawing the Duke magnified

You used the drawImage() method as follows:

```
gg.drawImage(MyImage,
            XMousePosOld,
            YMousePosOld,
            150,
            150,
            null);
```

Note that now drawImage() has six parameters, while in the mouseDrag() method you used a drawImage() method that had only four parameters. Some methods in Java can have the same function name, and yet have a different number of parameters. Java will notice how many parameters you have supplied and execute the appropriate method accordingly. A method that can be executed in different ways depending on the number of parameters that it has is called an *overloaded* method.

The fourth and fifth parameters of the drawImage() method indicate the size of the image. You supplied 150 as the fourth parameter (the width parameter) and 150 as the fifth parameter (the height parameter). This means that T1.GIF will be placed with its upper-left corner at the coordinates specified by the second and third parameters of drawImage(), and the image will be stretched over an area 150 pixels wide and 150 pixels high.

WHAT ABOUT ANIMATION?

Animation is the process of displaying images in a rapid sequence, creating the illusion that the objects shown in the images are moving. You can perform animation with Java by simply displaying one image after the other. For example, if you display the following sequence of images:

```
T1.GIF
T2.GIF
T3.GIF
```

it will look as if the Duke is waving hello.

Animation examples are not provided in this chapter, because before you can perform animation you must learn about threads and thread-related topics, which are discussed in the next chapter.

Animation, Threads, Extracting Tag Values, and Other Java Tricks

Displaying a sequence of images

Threads in Java: making the most of multitasking

Example 1: executing runnable applets

Example 2: extracting the values of HTML tags

Example 3: designing an applet to display an animation

Chapter 7

In Chapter 6 you learned how to draw and display graphic images using Java. In this chapter you'll learn how to perform animation. This requires understanding tasks that underlie the use of animation, such as implementing threads and extracting the values from HTML tags.

DISPLAYING A SEQUENCE OF IMAGES

An animation is a rapid sequence of images, much like a paper flipbook. To create animations using a computer, one might expect to begin with a program that looks like this:

```
// Animation starts here
A statement that displays image #1
A statement that displays image #2
A statement that displays image #3
…
…
…
// Animation ends here
```

The problem with the above program is that nowadays computers are very fast, and in this case the sequence of images would be displayed so quickly that the viewer wouldn't see individual images.

You might think that introducing a delay in between the images would solve this problem:

```
// Animation  starts here
A statement that displays image #1
   delay (so that image #1 stays on the screen for the
   duration of the delay).
A statement that displays image #2
   delay (so that image #2 stays on the screen for the
   duration of the delay).
A statement that displays image #3
   delay (so that image #3 stays on the screen for the
   duration of the delay).

...
...
...
// Animation ends here
```

The method used in this program segment is called *linear programming*—that is, the program moves from statement to statement in a linear manner. The problem with linear programming is that once the program starts, there is no way the user can stop it. So if the animation show takes five minutes, you have just forced your user to stay tuned to your show for five minutes! Naturally, it is not a good idea to force users to do anything. This is true for any program, and especially for Java programs that are executed over the Internet. (Imagine this: A user logs into your Web page, which contains an animation. Your user is now stuck for a full five minutes, even if he or she has visited before. Can you imagine the aggravation this would create?)

A better way to impress your users is to display animation in the background. That is, your HTML page may contain an animation show, but it does not prevent users from doing other things—for example, while the animation is in progress, your user can scroll around your HTML page. To accomplish background animation, you must use the threading capability of Java.

THREADS IN JAVA: MAKING THE MOST OF MULTITASKING

With Java, you can execute applications in threads. A *thread* is a program that is executed without monopolizing the computer. Let's say you're displaying an HTML page that has an applet in it. The applet executes an animation thread. While the animation thread is going on, the user is able to use the mouse to perform other tasks. In other words, the animation show does not monopolize the PC's resources. A program capable of implementing threads is sometimes referred to as a *multitasking* program, because each thread is considered a task, and the multitasking program is capable of performing several tasks simultaneously.

Java programs can execute several threads simultaneously although the word *simultaneously* is a bit misleading. As you know, most PCs have a single CPU, and that CPU is capable of executing one instruction at a time. Let's say that two threads are being executed "simultaneously" on a PC that has a single CPU in it. In reality, the CPU executes some statements of the first thread, then some statements of the second thread, then additional statements of the first thread, and so on. To the user it looks as if two threads are being executed simultaneously.

Let's take a look again at an example where an animation show is executed as a thread. Furthermore, assume that the animation show is executed in an endless loop. It displays image 1, image 2, and image 3, and then it starts all over again. Because the animation is performed as a thread, the user is not stuck watching it. Why? Because although to the user it may look as if the entire CPU is dedicated to performing the animation, the CPU is still taking care of other tasks. For example, the user can click a button that causes the animation to stop, the user can scroll around the HTML page where the animation occurs, and so on.

EXAMPLE 1: EXECUTING RUNNABLE APPLETS

In this example you'll design and implement an applet that executes a thread. This means that once the applet is executed, the user does not have to wait for the applet to be terminated, and the user can terminate execution of the applet at any time.

1 Create the C:\Java\MyDemo\MyThread directory. This is the directory where you'll save the files of this example.

2 Use your text editor program to create the MyThread.html file, and save the file as a text file inside the C:\Java\MyDemp\MyThread directory. Type the following code inside the MyThread.html file:

```
<html>

<title>MyThread.html</title>

<body>
```

```
<h1>This is the MyThread.html page.</h1>


<applet code="MyThread.class" width=200 height=200>
</applet>

<hr>

This HTML page uses the MyThread.class applet.

<hr>

</body>
</html>
```

3 Use your text editor to create the MyThread.java file, and save it as a text file inside the C:\Java\MyDemo\MyThread directory. Type the following code inside the MyThread.java file:

```java
// MyThread.java

import java.applet.*;
import java.awt.*;
import java.awt.peer.*;
import java.awt.image.*;
import java.io.*;
import java.net.*;
import java.util.*;

public class MyThread extends Applet implements Runnable
{


Thread gMyThread;

int giCurrentNumber;

    public void paint(Graphics g)
    {

    g.drawString("Hi, I'm the MyThread applet. " + giCurrentNumber,
             10,
             20);

    giCurrentNumber = giCurrentNumber + 1;
```

```
        if (giCurrentNumber == 1000)
          {

          giCurrentNumber = 0;

          }// end of if()

    } // end of paint()


    public void start()
    {

    gMyThread = new Thread(this);
    gMyThread.start();

    }// end of start()

    public void stop()
    {

    gMyThread.stop();

    }// end of stop()

    public void run()
    {
    while (true)
          {
          try
            {

            Thread.currentThread().sleep(10);

            } catch (InterruptedException e){}

            repaint();

          } // end of while()

      }//  end of run()

  }// end of class declaration
```

4 Execute a DOS shell, use the JavaC.exe compiler to compile the My-
  Thread.java file to create the MyThread.class file, and then execute the
  AppletViewer program to display the MyThread.html page.

The window shown in Figure 7.1 will appear. As you can see, the applet serves as a counter that counts from 0 to 1000. When the counter reaches 1000, it starts all over again at 0.

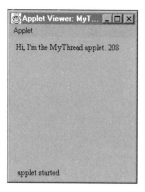

Figure 7.1: The MyThread applet continuously displays numbers.

The important thing to note is that the counter is working as a thread. The counter does not monopolize the system, and the user can stop the counter at any time (for example, when using the AppletViewer, the user can select Close from the Applet menu). When the applet is used inside an HTML page and viewed with a Web browser program that can execute Java applets, the user will see the counter working, but will nevertheless be able to scroll up and down the page and perform other tasks with the mouse.

CREATING A RUNNABLE APPLET

When implementing an applet in a thread, you declare the class as follows:

```
public class MyThread extends Applet implements Runnable
{

    ...
    ...
    ...

}
```

Note the words *implements Runnable* on the first line of the class declaration.

You declared the gMyThread variable as follows:

```
Thread gMyThread;
```

This statement declares gMyThread as a variable of type Thread. As you might have guessed, a variable of type Thread holds a number that represents the thread (think of this as the ID number of the thread).

You also declared the giCurrentNumber variable to be an integer:

```
int giCurrentNumber;
```

As you'll soon see, giCurrentNumber is the variable of the counter, and changes its value from 1 to 1000.

THE START() METHOD

Java executes the start() method automatically whenever the applet is started. When implementing a Runnable applet, you have to write code that starts the thread. This code is typed inside the start() method as follows:

```
public void start()
   {

  gMyThread = new Thread(this);
  gMyThread.start();

  }// end of start()
```

The code inside the start() method sets the value of gMyThread as follows:

```
gMyThread = new Thread(this);
```

In the preceding statement a new thread is created, and the variable gMy-Thread is set to a value that represents the new thread. Then the gMyThread thread is started by applying the start() method to gMyThread as follows:

```
gMyThread.start();
```

At this point in the program, the thread is started.

THE STOP() METHOD

The start() method may be considered an overhead code that is needed when implementing Runnable Java applets. Another necessary overhead code is the stop() method. The stop() method is automatically executed whenever the user stops the applet.

Here is the code of the stop() method:

```
public void stop()
   {

  gMyThread.stop();
```

```
}// end of stop()
```

This code causes the thread to be terminated.

THE RUN() METHOD

So far you have learned that when implementing Runnable applets, you have to include the start() method and the stop() method. The last overhead code you need is the run() method. The run() method is what makes the desired action take place. Typically, the run() method in a Runnable applet will look as follows:

```
public void run()
    {
    while (true)
        {
        try
          {

          Thread.currentThread().sleep(10);

          } catch (InterruptedException e){}

          repaint();

        } // end of while()

    }//  end of run()
```

Two sections you should pay special attention to in the run() method are the sleep() method and the code that appears after the catch statement.

The sleep() method   Here is the statement that executes the sleep() method:

```
Thread.currentThread().sleep(10);
```

This statement causes the currently executing thread to sleep, or stop executing, for the amount of time specified in the parameter. You specified 10 as the parameter of sleep(). This means that the currently executed thread will sleep for 10 milliseconds. So if the thread is performing an animation, for example, the code of the thread will display an image, then the thread will stop executing for 10 milliseconds. This means that the image will be displayed for 10 milliseconds on the monitor. Then the thread will continue and display the next image. Once the second image is displayed, the thread will again sleep and display that image for another 10 milliseconds before it once again continues executing, and so on. Note that for animation sequences, the sleep time between images should be set at between 400 and 1,000 milliseconds, not 10 milliseconds.

The code executed by the applet when the MyThread applet is not in sleep mode is

```
repaint();
```

In the case of the MyThread applet, you have only the repaint() method executed when the applet is not in sleep mode, but of course you can add other statements that you wish the applet to execute.

To summarize, when implementing a Runnable applet you must do the following:

- ▶ Write the start() method
- ▶ Write the stop() method
- ▶ Write the run() method
- ▶ When writing the run() method, write two customized sections: the sleep() statement, which determines the amount of time that the applet will not execute code; and customized code that should be executed when the applet is not in sleep mode

When the applet is in sleep mode, the computer is available to perform other tasks. If, for example, a user clicks the mouse to scroll down the HTML page while the applet is in sleep mode, the HTML page will scroll down. If the user clicks the mouse while the applet is not in a sleep mode, the clicking event is stored as a *pending event*. Eventually, the applet will finish executing the paint() method—which is being executed due to the execution of the re-paint() method—and the applet will enter sleep mode. At this point, the pending event will be executed.

THE PAINT() EVENT OF THE MYTHREAD APPLET

In between the sleeps, the applet executes the repaint() method, which causes the execution of the paint() method:

```
public void paint(Graphics g)
    {

    g.drawString("Hi, I'm the MyThread applet. " + giCurrentNumber,
                10,
                20);

    giCurrentNumber = giCurrentNumber + 1;
```

```
    if (giCurrentNumber == 1000)
       {

       giCurrentNumber = 0;

       }// end of if()

    } // end of paint()
```

The drawString() method displays a string at a location 10 pixels from the left edge of the apple and 20 pixels from the top edge of the applet:

```
g.drawString("Hi, I'm the MyThread applet. " + giCurrentNumber,
            10,
            20);
```

The displayed string is *Hi, I'm the MyThread applet.*, followed by the value of the giCurrentNumber integer. Upon starting the applet, giCurrentNumber is initialized to 0. So the first time the paint() method is executed, the following string is executed:

```
Hi, I'm the MyThread applet. 0
```

The next statement inside the paint() method increases the value of giCurrentNumber by 1:

```
giCurrentNumber = giCurrentNumber + 1;
```

An if statement is then executed to examine whether giCurrentNumber is equal to 1,000:

```
if (giCurrentNumber === 1000)
       {

       giCurrentNumber = 0;

       }// end of if()
```

If giCurrentNumber is equal to 1,000, the statement under the if statement is executed, and this statement sets the value of giCurrentNumber back to 0.

The first time the paint() method is executed, giCurrentNumber is set to 0+1=1. On the next execution of the paint() method, giCurrentNumber is equal to 1, because it was declared at the beginning of the MyThread class declaration, not inside the paint() method. This means that giCurrentNumber maintains its value for as long as the applet is running. On the second execution of the paint() method, giCurrentNumber is set to 1+1=2.

As this process continues, the paint() method giCurrentNumber is increased by 1 with each execution. Eventually, giCurrentNumber is equal to 1000, and the statement under the if is executed. This causes giCurrentNumber to be set back to 0, and now the counter starts counting from 0 all over again.

THE INIT() METHOD

The MyThread applet that you implemented starts counting from 0. But what if you need the counter to count from 20 to 1,000 instead of 0 to 1,000? To accomplish this, you can use the init() method. First add the init() method to the MyThread class, inside the MyThread.java file. Here is the code of the init() method:

```
public void init()
   {

   giCurrentNumber = 20;

   } // end of init()
```

Java executes the init() method automatically whenever the applet is created. This is your chance to execute code that performs various initializations. In this example, you use the init() method to initialize the giCurrentNumber variable to 20. Remember, the init() method will be executed before all the other methods. So when the paint() method is executed for the first time, giCurrentNumber will already be set to 20.

When the counter reaches 1,000, you want the applet to start counting again from 20. This means that you have to change the statement under the if statement inside the paint() method as follows:

```
if (giCurrentNumber == 1000)
   {

   giCurrentNumber = 20;

   }// end of if()
```

Now, when the giCurrentNumber variable reaches 1,000, the statement under the if statement will set the value of the giCurrentNumber variable back to 20, not 0.

Compile and then execute the applet, and notice that now the counter counts from 20 to 1,000.

CHANGING THE SPEED OF THE COUNTER

The parameter of the sleep() method determines the amount of time that the applet is in sleep mode.

To change the speed of the counter so that the counter will work more slowly, use 1,000 milliseconds as the parameter of the sleep() method:

```
Thread.currentThread().sleep(1000);
```

Now the applet will execute the repaint() method, then sleep for 1,000 milliseconds (1 second). In each count, the current number of the counter will remain on the screen for a full 1 second before the counter is increased again.

EXAMPLE 2: EXTRACTING THE VALUES OF HTML TAGS

As you saw in the preceding section, one way to increase or decrease the speed of the counter is by simply changing the parameter of the sleep() method. This, of course, means that you have to use JavaC.exe to compile the MyThread.java file again. However, your user does not have access to the MyThread.java file—and even if you supplied users with the MyThread.java file, you couldn't expect them to use JavaC.exe to recompile it! Nevertheless, in many cases you do want to let users have some control over your applets' programmability. For example, you may want users to be able to determine the speed of the counter.

The following example illustrates how you can let users set the speed of the counter without the need to recompile the applet by adding a param tag to an HTML page.

Use your text editor to modify the MyThread.html file so that it looks like this:

```
<html>

<title>MyThread.html</title>

<body>

<h1>This is the MyThread.html page.</h1>

<applet code="MyThread.class" width=200 height=200>
<param name=CounterSpeed Value="1000">
</applet>

<hr>
```

```
This HTML page uses the MyThread.class applet.

<hr>

</body>
</html>
```

As you can see, you added the param tag. Before elaborating on the param tag, let's use the AppletViewer to execute the MyThread.class applet and the modified MyThread.html file.

Note that the applet still works just as it worked with the original MyThread.class applet. In other words, the modification that you made to the MyThread.html file does not have any effect on operability. This makes sense, because you haven't yet modified the code of the MyThread.java file to make use of the param tag that you've added to the MyThread.html file. The applet doesn't collapse, it simply ignores the param tag that it finds inside the MyThread.html file.

Now you'll learn how to extract the value of the param tag, and make use of it:

1 Modify the MyThread.java file so that it looks like the following:

```java
// MyThread.java
import java.applet.*;
import java.awt.*;
import java.awt.peer.*;
import java.awt.image.*;
import java.io.*;
import java.net.*;
import java.util.*;

public class MyThread extends Applet implements Runnable
{

Thread gMyThread;

int giCurrentNumber;

int     giCounterSpeed;
String gsSpeedFromHTML;

public void init()
    {

    giCurrentNumber = 20;
```

```
gsSpeedFromHTML = getParameter("CounterSpeed");

giCounterSpeed =
    Integer.valueOf(gsSpeedFromHTML).intValue();

} // end of init()


public void paint(Graphics g)
{

  // g.drawString("Hi, I'm the MyThread applet. " +
giCurrentNumber,
  //            10,
  //            20);


    g.drawString("Extracted speed: "+
                gsSpeedFromHTML +
                " Counter: "+ giCurrentNumber,
                10,
                20);

giCurrentNumber = giCurrentNumber + 1;

        if (giCurrentNumber == 1000)
           {

           giCurrentNumber = 20;

           }// end of if()


} // end of paint()


public void start()
{

gMyThread = new Thread(this);
gMyThread.start();

}// end of start()

public void stop()
{

gMyThread.stop();
```

```
}// end of stop()

public void run()
{
while (true)
      {
      try
       {

       // Thread.currentThread().sleep(10);
       Thread.currentThread().sleep(giCounterSpeed);

       } catch (InterruptedException e){}

       repaint();

      } // end of while()

   }//  end of run()

}// end of class declaration
```

2 Use JavaC.exe to compile the modified MyThread.java file.

3 Use the AppletViewer program to execute MyThread.html.

Notice that now the applet displays the extracted speed (see Figure 7.2).
And, of course, the counter is now counting at a slower speed, increasing every
1,000 milliseconds.

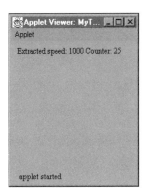

Figure 7.2: The applet displays the extracted speed value.

THE GETPARAMETER() METHOD

At the beginning of the class declaration you declared two additional variables:

```
int    giCounterSpeed;
String gsSpeedFromHTML;
```

That is, you declared an integer and a string, and these variables are accessible by any method of the class.

Take a look at the modified init() method:

```
public void init()
   {

   giCurrentNumber = 20;


   gsSpeedFromHTML = getParameter("CounterSpeed");

   giCounterSpeed =
      Integer.valueOf(gsSpeedFromHTML).intValue();


   } // end of init()
```

The getParameter() method extracts the value mentioned in the HTML tag.

Inside the HTML file you have:

```
<param name=CounterSpeed Value="1000">
```

You supply *CounterSpeed* as the parameter of the getParameter() method, and the getParameter() returns the string *1000*.

Inside the MyThread.java file you need the speed value as an integer, not as a string, so you convert the string to an integer as follows:

```
giCounterSpeed =
      Integer.valueOf(gsSpeedFromHTML).intValue();
```

At this point in the program, the gsSpeedFromHTML contains a string that holds the string mentioned in the HTML file. The giCounterSpeed variable holds an integer that corresponds to the extracted string from the HTML file.

The modified paint() method draws a string as follows:

```
g.drawString("Extracted speed: "+
             gsSpeedFromHTML +
             " Counter: "+ giCurrentNumber,
             10,
             20);
```

For example, if gsSpeedFromHTML is equal to 1,000 and giCurrentNumber is equal to 25, then the following string is displayed:

```
Extracted speed: 1000 Counter: 25
```

Inside the run() method you changed the sleep() statement as follows:

```
Thread.currentThread().sleep(giCounterSpeed);
```

Accordingly, if the tag inside the HTML file indicates that the speed is 1,000, the parameter of the sleep() method will be equal to 1,000.

Now you can experiment with different speeds by simply modifying the values of the speed tag inside the HTML file, with no need to recompile the applet.

Currently, the applet tag includes a single param tag:

```
<applet code="MyThread.class" width=200 height=200>
<param name=CounterSpeed Value="1000">
</applet>
```

You can add additional tags. For example, suppose that you want the counter to start counting from a certain number, and you want this number to be programmable from within the HTML page. You can add additional param tags to the MyThread.html file as follows:

```
<applet code="MyThread.class" width=200 height=200>
<param name=CounterSpeed Value="1000">
<param name=StartingFrom Value="100">
</applet>
```

You'll then have to modify the MyThread.java file so that the value of Starting-From param tag is extracted, and the extracted value is then used as the starting number of the counter. You can add other param tags to the HTML file in a similar manner.

EXAMPLE 3: DESIGNING AN APPLET TO DISPLAY AN ANIMATION

Equipped with this know-how about threading in Java, you can now design an applet that displays an animation. In this example you'll implement the MyAnim applet, an applet that demonstrates how you can deploy animation shows with Java.

1 Create the directory c:\Java\MyDemo\MyAnim. This is the directory where you'll save the files used in this example.

2 Use your text editor to create the MyAnim.html file, and save it as a
text file inside the C:\MyJava\MyDemo\MyAnim directory. Inside the
MyAnim.html file, type the following code:

```
<html>

<title>MyAnim.html</title>

<body>

<h1>This is the MyAnim.html page.</h1>

<applet code="MyAnim.class" width=200 height=200>
</applet>

<hr>

This HTML page uses the MyAnim.class applet.

<hr>

</body>
</html>
```

The MyAnim.html page uses the MyAnim.class applet.

The MyAnim.java file that you'll create in this example requires several GIF
files. Now copy the required GIF files:

1 Copy the *.GIF files that reside inside the C:\Java\Demo\Animator\
Images\Duke to the C:\Java\MyDemo\MyAnim directory. You'll practice
with the GIF files that come with Java in this example.

2 Use your text editor to create the MyAnim.java file, and save it as a
text file inside the C:\MyJava\MyDemo\MyAnim directory. Inside the
MyAnim.java file type the following code:

```
// MyAnim.java

import java.applet.*;
import java.awt.*;
import java.awt.peer.*;
import java.awt.image.*;
import java.io.*;
import java.net.*;
import java.util.*;

public class MyAnim extends Applet implements Runnable
```

```
{

Thread gAnimationThread;
int    gFrameNumber;

    public void init()
    {

    gFrameNumber = 1;

    }// end of init()


    public void paint(Graphics g)
    {

    g.drawString ("Frame Number: " + gFrameNumber,
                  10,
                  20);


    gFrameNumber = gFrameNumber + 1;
    if (gFrameNumber == 11 )
        {
        gFrameNumber = 1;
        }

    }// end of paint()


    public void start()
    {

    gAnimationThread = new Thread(this);
    gAnimationThread.start();

    }// end of start()

    public void stop()
    {

    gAnimationThread.stop();

    }// end of stop()
```

```
public void run()
{
while (true)
      {
      try {
          Thread.currentThread().sleep(500);
          } catch (InterruptedException e){}

      repaint();
      }// end of while()

  }//  end of run()

}// end of class declaration
```

3 Use JavaC.exe to compile the MyAnim.java file, then use the Applet-Viewer program to execute the MyAnim.html page.

The window shown in Figure 7.3 will now appear. As you can see, the applet displays the text Frame Number: N, where *N* is a number between 1 and 10. The frame number changes every second.

Figure 7.3: Displaying the frame number with the MyAnim applet

There is no animation here yet, but the essence of the animation has been implemented. All that you have to do now is add code to the MyAnim.java file that displays images instead of text. You'll do that in the following sections.

USING A VECTOR TO HOLD ANIMATION IMAGES

As stated previously, an animation is a sequence of images. Typically, you store these images in either a *vector* or an *array*. As our first example, we'll demonstrate how images are stored in a vector.

At the beginning of the MyAnim class declaration (inside the MyAnim.java file), add the declaration of a variable called *TheImages* of type Vector as follows:

```
public class MyAnim extends Applet implements Runnable
{

Thread gAnimationThread;
int    gFrameNumber;

Vector    TheImages = new Vector(20);
...
...
...
} // End of class declaration
```

A vector is very similar in concept to an array. You declared the TheImages vector as one that can hold a maximum of 20 elements. (You'll actually store only 10 images in the vector, but you can set the maximum number of elements to a larger number in case you decide to use more than 10 images for the animation in the future.)

Add code to the init() method inside the MyAnim.java file so that the init() method looks as follows:

```
public void init()
    {

    gFrameNumber = 1;

    int      i;
    String si;
    Image TempImage;

    for (i=0; i<10; i++)
        {
        si = String.valueOf(i+1);
        TempImage = getImage(getCodeBase(), "T"+si+".gif" );
        TheImages.addElement(TempImage);
        }

    }// end of init()
```

You declared an integer, a string, and a variable called TempImage of type Image:

```
int      i;
String  si;
Image    TempImage;
```

Then execute a for() loop.

```
for (i=0; i<10; i++)
  {
  …
  … The body of the for() loop
  …
  }
```

The for() loop starts with the variable i equal to 0, as specified in the first section of the parenthesis of the for() loop statement. Then the body of the for() loop is executed. After the execution of the statements that reside inside the body of the for() loop, the third section of statements inside the parenthesis of the for() loop is executed. Because you specified i++ as the third section inside the parenthesis of the for() loop, i is increased by 1. So now i is equal to 0+1=1. The second section of the parenthesis of the for() loop checks to see if i is still less than 10. Because currently i is equal to 1, the body of the for() loop is executed again. Now the body of the for() loop is executed with i equal to 1. When the statements inside the body of the for() loop are completed, i is again increased by 1. So now i is equal to 1+1=2. Because i is still less than 10, the body of the for() loop is executed again. This process continues until i is no longer less than 10. When i is equal to 10 the for() loop is terminated. Putting it all together, the for() loop was executed 10 times. The first time i was equal to 0, the second time i was equal to 1, and so on. The last time the body of the for() loop was executed, i was equal to 9.

Now let's see what's going on inside the body of the for() loop that you executed 10 times. The string *si* is set as follows:

```
si = String.valueOf(i+1);
```

When the for() loop was executed for the first time, *si* was set to the string 0+1=1. When the for() loop was executed for the second time, si was set to 1+1=2. The last time the for() loop was executed, si was set to 9+1=10.

The variable TempImage is then assigned with the path and file name of a GIF file as follows:

```
TempImage = getImage(getCodeBase(), "T"+si+".gif" );
```

When the for() loop was executed for the first time (when si was equal to 1), TempImage was set to T1.GIF. When the for() loop was executed for the second time, si equal to 2, so TempImage was set to T2.GIF. In the last iteration of the for() loop, TempImage was set to T10.GIF.

The last statement that you typed inside the body of the for() loop was as follows:

```
TheImages.addElement(TempImage);
```

You used the addElement() method to add elements to the TheImages vector. During the first execution of the for() loop, T1.GIF was added to the TheImages vector. During the second execution of the for() loop, T2.GIF was added to the vector, and so on.

After the for() loop is terminated, the TheImages vector is composed of the following elements:

```
Element number 0: T1.GIF
Element number 1: T2.GIF
Element number 2: T3.GIF
Element number 3: T4.GIF
Element number 4: T5.GIF
Element number 5: T6.GIF
Element number 6: T7.GIF
Element number 7: T8.GIF
Element number 8: T9.GIF
Element number 9: T10.GIF
```

Displaying the images The last thing you have to do to complete the animation is add code inside the paint() method that displays the images. First, modify the paint() method of the MyAnim class inside the MyAnim.java file so that the paint() method looks as follows:

```
public void paint(Graphics g)
    {

    // g.drawString ("Frame Number: " + gFrameNumber,
    //                 10,
    //                 20);

    String si;
    si = String.valueOf(gFrameNumber);
    g.drawString ("Now showing filename: " + "T"+si+".GIF",
                    10,
                    50);

    Image CurrentImage;
    CurrentImage =
         (Image) TheImages.elementAt(gFrameNumber-1);

    g.drawImage(CurrentImage,
```

```
                               30,
                               70,
                               null);


        gFrameNumber = gFrameNumber + 1;
        if (gFrameNumber == 11 )
           {
           gFrameNumber = 1;
           }

     }// end of paint()
```

The code that you typed declares the string si:

```
String si;
```

Note that because you declare si inside the paint() method, the *si* variable is known only inside the paint() method. Other methods do not have access to the si variable. In fact, you already declared a variable called *si* inside the init() method. But it is very important to understand that the si of the init() method has nothing to do with the si variable of the paint() method.

The si string is then set to a string that corresponds to the gFrameNumber integer:

```
si = String.valueOf(gFrameNumber);
```

When gFrameNumber is equal to 1, si is equal to the string 1. When gFrame-Number is equal to 2, si is equal to the string 2, and so on.

The drawString() method is then executed to display a string:

```
g.drawString ("Now showing filename: " + "T"+si+".GIF",
                  10,
                  50);
```

When si is equal to 1, the following string is displayed:

```
Now showing filename: T1.GIF
```

When si is equal to 2, the following string is displayed:

```
Now showing filename: T2.GIF
```

A variable called *CurrentImage* of type *Image* is declared:

```
Image CurrentImage;
```

Then the CurrentImage variable is set as follows:

```
CurrentImage =
        (Image) TheImages.elementAt(gFrameNumber-1);
```

elementAt() is a method that returns the element mentioned as the parameter of the elementAt() method. You preceded the elementAt() method with a period and the name of the vector TheImages, so when gFrameNumber is equal to 1, the element 1-1=0 of the TheImages vector will be assigned to the CurrentImage variable. When gFrameNumber is equal to 2, element number 1 of TheImages vector will be assigned to the CurrentImage variable, and so on.

Note that the text Image surrounded by parenthesis is used:

```
CurrentImage =
        (Image) TheImages.elementAt(gFrameNumber-1);
```

As it turns out, the elementAt() method returns the value of the vector. But what is the type of the returned value from the elementAt() method? Is it an integer? Is it a string? Is it a variable that represents an image? Vectors can contain many things. As such, the returned value from the elementAt() method is unknown. What is known is that the returned value from elementAt() must be a value of type Image, because you are assigning the returned value to the variable CurrentImage, which is of type Image. What you did is apply *casting*. By prefixing the returned value of elementAt() with (Image), you are telling Java that it is okay to assign the returned value of elementAt() to the CurrentImage variable. Furthermore, the casting is telling Java to format the returned value so that the CurrentImage variable will be able to store the value of the returned value.

Now draw the image by applying the drawImage() method:

```
g.drawImage(CurrentImage,
                30,
                70,
                null);
```

When gFrameNumber is equal to 1, the drawImage() method displays the T1.GIF file. When gFrameNumber is equal to 2, the drawImage() method displays the T2.GIF file, and so on.

You then increase the value of gFrameNumber by 1:

```
gFrameNumber = gFrameNumber + 1;
```

The last thing that is executed inside the paint() method is an if statement:

```
if (gFrameNumber == 11 )
    {
```

```
gFrameNumber = 1;
}
```

The if statement ensures that gFrameNumber does not exceed 10. In fact, if gFrameNumber is equal to 11, the statement under the if statement sets the value of gFrameNumber back to 1.

Now let's take a final look at the MyAnim class:

1 A thread is executed. The thread sleeps for 500 milliseconds. Then the repaint() method is executed.

2 The repaint() method causes the paint() method to be executed. Because currently gFrameNumber is equal to 1, the code inside the paint() method displays the T1.GIF picture, and this code also increases the value of gFrameNumber to 1+1=2.

3 The thread is now in sleep mode for 500 milliseconds, so T1.GIF is displayed on the screen for 500 milliseconds.

4 The thread is executed again, which means that the repaint() method is executed again. Because now gFrameNumber is equal to 2, the code inside the paint() method displays the T2.GIF, and then the thread enters sleep mode for 500 milliseconds. Now T2.GIF is displayed for 500 milliseconds.

5 This process continues until gFrameNumber is equal to 11, when the code inside the paint() method causes the value of gFrameNumber to be set back to 1.

When the animation is all put together, the paint() method displays the following sequence of pictures:

```
T1.GIF (for 500 milliseconds)
T2.GIF (for 500 milliseconds)
T3.GIF (for 500 milliseconds)
...
...

...
T10.GIF (for 500 milliseconds)
T1.GIF (for 500 milliseconds)
T2.GIF (for 500 milliseconds)
T3.GIF (for 500 milliseconds)
...
...

...
```

Because the applet is implemented as a Runnable applet and is in sleep mode most of the time, the user is able to perform other tasks while the animation is in progress.

Use JavaC.exe to compile the MyAnim.java file and create the MyAnim.class file. Use the AppletViewer program to execute the MyAnim.html page. As you can see, the applet displays the animation. Figure 7.4 shows the animation when the T6.GIF picture is displayed.

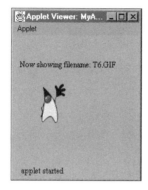

Figure 7.4: The animation, shown at the time the T6.GIF image is displayed

Note: The first time the animation is progressing, no pictures are displayed. The images are displayed only after gFrameNumber has already been equal to 10, and then has been set back to 1.

Note: Typically, you will not display the message *Now showing filename:* during the animation. The only reason you were instructed to display this string is to help you follow the sequence of the animation during development and experimentation.

USING AN ARRAY TO HOLD ANIMATION IMAGES

In the previous section you used a vector to hold the images that are displayed during an animation show. Using an array is an alternative to using a vector. In the following example you'll create the MyAnim2 class, an applet that performs an identical task to that accomplished by the MyAnim applet. The only reason we are introducing the MyAnim2 applet is to demonstrate the use of arrays in Java.

1 Create the C:\Java\MyDemo\MyAnim2 directory.

2 Copy the GIF files that reside inside the C:\Java\MyDemo\Animator\Images\Duke directory to the C:\Java\MyDemo\MyAnim2 directory.

3 Use your text editor to create the MyAnim2.html file, and save as a regular text file in the C:\Java\MyDemo\MyAnim2 directory. Type the following code inside the MyAnim2.html file:

```
<html>

<title>MyAnim2.html</title>

<body>

<h1>This is the MyAnim2.html page.</h1>


<applet code="MyAnim2.class" width=200 height=200>
</applet>


<hr>

This HTML page uses the MyAnim2.class applet.

<hr>

</body>
</html>
```

4 Use your text editor to create the MyAnim2.java file, and save it as a regular text file in the C:\Java\MyDemo\MyAnim2 directory. Type the following code inside the MyAnim2.java file:

```
// MyAnim.java

import java.applet.*;
import java.awt.*;
import java.awt.peer.*;
import java.awt.image.*;
import java.io.*;
import java.net.*;
import java.util.*;

public class MyAnim2 extends Applet implements Runnable
{

Thread   gAnimationThread = null;
```

```
int       gFrameNumber;

int       gSpeed = 1;

Image     TheImages[];


    public void init()
    {

    gFrameNumber = 1;


    TheImages = new Image[20];
    for (int i = 1; i < 11; i++)
        {
        TheImages[i-1] =
        getImage(getDocumentBase(), "T" + i + ".gif");
        } // end of for()


    }// end of init()


    public void paint(Graphics g)
    {


    String si;

    si = String.valueOf(gFrameNumber);
    g.drawString ("Now showing filename: " + "T"+si+".GIF",
                10,
                50);

     g.drawImage(TheImages[gFrameNumber-1],
                30,
                70,
                null);

    gFrameNumber = gFrameNumber + 1;
    if (gFrameNumber == 11  )
        {
        gFrameNumber = 1;
        gSpeed=500;
        }
```

```
}// end of paint()


public void start()
{
gAnimationThread = new Thread(this);
gAnimationThread.start();
}// end of start()

public void stop()
{
gAnimationThread.stop();
}// end of stop()



public void run()
{
while (true)
    {
    try {
        Thread.currentThread().sleep(gSpeed);
        } catch (InterruptedException e){}
     repaint();
    }// end of while()
}//  end of run()



}// end of class declaration
```

5 Use JavaC.exe to compile the MyAnim2.java file and create the MyAnim2.class file. Use AppletViewer to execute the MyAnim2.html file.

6 Verify that the images T1.GIF through T10.GIF are displayed as an animation.

Declaring an array of images   At the beginning of the MyAnim2 class you declared the TheImages array of images as follows:

```
public class MyAnim2 extends Applet implements Runnable
{

Thread    gAnimationThread = null;
int       gFrameNumber;
```

```
int      gSpeed = 1;

Image    TheImages[];

...

...

...
}
```

TheImages[] is an array of type Image, so TheImages[0] is the first element of the array, and this element can hold a variable that contains an image. TheImages[1] is the second element of TheImages[], and so on.

Also note that a variable gSpeed of type int was declared, and this variable was set to 1.

Filling the array of images   Inside the init() method you filled the array of images as follows:

```
public void init()
    {

    gFrameNumber = 1;


    TheImages = new Image[20];
    for (int i = 1; i < 11; i++)
        {
        TheImages[i-1] =
            getImage(getDocumentBase(), "T" + i + ".gif");
        } // end of for()

    }// end of init()
```

For example, when i is equal to 1, the first element of TheImages (TheImages[0]) is filled with T1.GIF:

```
TheImages[1-1] =
        getImage(getDocumentBase(), "T" + 1 + ".gif");
```

Displaying elements of the array   Inside the paint() method you display the elements of the array of images. Here is the statement that draws the image:

```
g.drawImage(TheImages[gFrameNumber-1],
                30,
                70,
                null);
```

The first parameter of drawImage() is TheImages[gFrameNumber-1]. So when gFrameNumber is equal to 1, for example, the element that is being displayed is

```
TheImages[1-1]
```

That is, TheImages[0] element is being displayed. As you can see, the code of the MyAnim2 class is very similar to the code of the MyAnim class.

The paint() method is executed the first 10 times the applet is executed. However, the process of displaying the first 10 empty images occurs very quickly, because gSpeed is set to 1, and inside the run() method the sleep period is set to gSpeed:

```
Thread.currentThread().sleep(gSpeed);
```

Once the 10 empty images have been displayed, the if statement inside the paint() method sets gSpeed to 500:

```
gFrameNumber = gFrameNumber + 1;
if (gFrameNumber == 11 )
   {
   gFrameNumber = 1;
   gSpeed=500;
   }
```

From now on, the images will be displayed and each image will stay on the screen for 500 milliseconds.

User Interface, Buttons, and Lists

EXAMPLE 1: PLACING A BUTTON INSIDE YOUR HTML PAGE

EXAMPLE 2: PLACING A LIST CONTROL INSIDE YOUR HTML PAGE

Chapter 8

Occasionally, you may want users to select an option from a list of choices on an HTML page. With Java, you can design applets that display standard user interface objects like buttons and lists. Once a user clicks a button, for example, your Java applet will execute the code that corresponds to that selection.

EXAMPLE 1: PLACING A BUTTON INSIDE YOUR HTML PAGE

In this example, you'll place a regular push button inside an applet.

1 Create the C:\Java\MyDemo\MyButton directory. You'll save the files created for this example into this directory.

2 Use your text editor to create the MyButton.html file, and save it as a text file into the C:\Java\MyDemo\MyButton directory. Inside the MyButton.html file, type the following code:

```
<html>

<title>MyButton.html</title>

<body>

<h1>This is the MyButton.html page.</h1>

<applet code=MyButton.class width=150 height=150>
```

149

```
</applet>

<hr>

This HTML page uses the MyButton.class applet.

<hr>

</body>
</html>
```

3 Use your text editor to create the MyButton.java file, and save it as a text file into the C:\Java\MyDemo\MyButton directory. Inside the My-Button.java file, type the following code:

```
// MyButton.java

import java.applet.*;
import java.awt.*;
import java.awt.peer.*;
import java.awt.image.*;
import java.io.*;
import java.net.*;
import java.util.*;

public class MyButton extends Applet
{

String sWhatWasPressed;

  public void init()
  {

  Panel p = new Panel();

  p.add(new Button("Me"));
  p.add(new Button("You"));
  p.add(new Button("Her"));
  p.add(new Button("His"));

  add("Select", p);

  resize(250,250);

  }// end of init()
```

```
public boolean action(Event evt, Object arg)
{

if ("Me".equals(arg))
   {
   sWhatWasPressed = "Me was pressed";
   }

if ("You".equals(arg))
   {
   sWhatWasPressed = "You was pressed";
   }

if ("Her".equals(arg))
   {
   sWhatWasPressed = "Her was pressed";
   }

if ("His".equals(arg))
   {
   sWhatWasPressed = "His was pressed";
   }

repaint();

return true;

}  // end of action()


public void paint(Graphics g)
{

g.drawString(sWhatWasPressed,
           75,
           75);


} // end of paint()


} // End of the class
```

4 Use JavaC.exe to compile the MyButton.java file and create the MyButton.class file. Use the AppletViewer program to execute the MyButton.html page. The AppletViewer will now display the MyButton applet, as shown in Figure 8.1. The applet has four push buttons in it: Me, You, Her, and His.

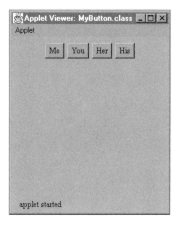

Figure 8.1: The MyButton applet, which contains four buttons: Me, You, Her, and His

5 Click the push buttons, and notice that the applet displays the name of the push button that you clicked (Figure 8.2).

Figure 8.2: When you click a button, the applet displays the name of the clicked button.

6 When you are finished experimenting with the MyButton applet, terminate the applet.

ADDING A NEW PANEL TO THE APPLET

At the beginning of the MyButton class, you declared the sWhatWasPressed string:

```
String sWhatWasPressed;
```

The sWhatWasPressed string will hold a string that represents the name of the clicked button.

Inside the init() method you declared a new panel as follows:

```
Panel p = new Panel();
```

A *panel* is an area inside the applet that is dedicated for placing objects, and in this example it is constructed with the default settings. From now on, your program can refer to the new panel as *p*.

The Me button can then be constructed as follows:

```
p.add(new Button("Me"));
```

The p panel now has a push button with *Me* as its caption. In a similar manner, you can now add the You, Her, and His buttons to the p panel:

```
p.add(new Button("You"));
  p.add(new Button("Her"));
  p.add(new Button("His"));
```

Now that the four push buttons are added to the p panel, you can add the panel component to the applet:

```
add("Select", p);
```

This statement adds the p panel, as specified by the second parameter of the add() method. The first parameter is a string that represents the name of the component that you are adding; however, in the MyButton applet the value of this string is not used.

THE RESIZE() METHOD

The last statement that you typed inside the init() method was the resize() method:

```
resize(250,250);
```

The resize() method sets a new size for the applet. In the preceding statement, the width of the applet is set to 250 pixels (the first parameter of the resize() method), and the height of the applet is also set to 250 pixels (the second parameter of the resize() method).

THE ACTION() METHOD

As its name implies, the action() method is where the action takes place. Inside the action() method you write code that examines whether or not any of the push buttons were pressed. In particular, pay attention to the arg parameter of the action() method:

```
public boolean action(Event evt, Object arg)
{

    . . .
    . . .
    . . .

}
```

Inside the action() method you use decision-making statements (for example, switch, if, or if…else) to determine if the push button was clicked.

Here is the if statement that examines if the Me button was pressed:

```
if ("Me".equals(arg))
    {
    sWhatWasPressed = "Me was pressed";
    }
```

With this code in place, if the user clicks the Me button, sWhatWasPressed is set to *Me was pressed.*

Likewise, here is the if statement that examines if the You button was pressed:

```
if ("You".equals(arg))
    {
    sWhatWasPressed = "You was pressed";
    }
```

You typed similar if statements for the Her and His push buttons.

Next, issue a repaint() statement:

```
repaint();
```

The repaint() statement causes the execution of the paint() method, and inside the paint() method you display the value of sWhatWasPressed. Of course, the only reason you are now displaying the value of sWhatWasPressed is to prove to yourself that the code you typed inside the action() method is working as expected.

The action() method must return true or false. Thus, the last statement you typed inside the action() method was

```
return true;
```

THE PAINT() METHOD

Inside the paint() method of the MyButton class you simply displayed the value of sWhatWasPressed:

```
public void paint(Graphics g)
  {

  g.drawString(sWhatWasPressed,
            75,
            75);

  } // end of paint()
```

EXAMPLE 2: PLACING A LIST CONTROL INSIDE YOUR HTML PAGE

A push button is just one example of a user interface control that you can incorporate into your Java applets. In the next example, you'll enhance the My-Button applet by adding a list control function to it. The user will be able to "open" the list and make a selection from it.

1 Use your text editor to modify the init() method of the MyButton class. After modification, the init() method should look as follows:

```
public void init()
  {

  Panel p = new Panel();

  p.add(new Button("Me"));
  p.add(new Button("You"));
  p.add(new Button("Her"));
  p.add(new Button("His"));

  Choice c;

  p.add(c = new Choice());
  c.addItem("My Choice");
  c.addItem("Her Choice");
  c.addItem("His Choice");
```

```
        c.addItem("Our Choice");
        c.addItem("Their Choice");

        add("Select", p);

        resize(250,250);

        }// end of init()
```

2 Use your text editor to modify the action() method of the MyButton class. After modifying the action() method, it should look as follows:

```
public boolean action(Event evt, Object arg)
{

if (evt.target instanceof Choice)
    {
    sWhatWasPressed = (String)arg;
    }
else
    {
    if ("Me".equals(arg))
        {
        sWhatWasPressed = "Me was pressed";
        }

    if ("You".equals(arg))
        {
        sWhatWasPressed = "You was pressed";
        }

    if ("Her".equals(arg))
        {
        sWhatWasPressed = "Her was pressed";
        }

    if ("His".equals(arg))
        {
        sWhatWasPressed = "His was pressed";
        }

    }// end of else


repaint();

return true;

}  // end of action()
```

3 Use JavaC.exe to compile the MyButton.java file and to create the MyButton.class file.

4 Use AppletViewer to execute the MyButton.HTML file. The window shown in Figure 8.3 will now appear. Now the applet contains the list control.

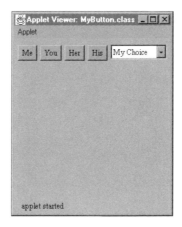

Figure 8.3: The MyButton applet with four buttons and one list control in it

5 Click the down-arrow icon of the list control. The MyButton applet will respond by dropping down the list of items, as shown in Figure 8.4.

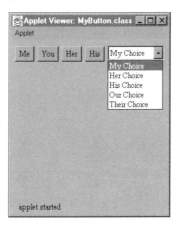

Figure 8.4: The drop-down list of the MyButton applet

6 Select the My Choice item from the list. MyButton will respond by displaying the selected item, as shown in Figure 8.5.

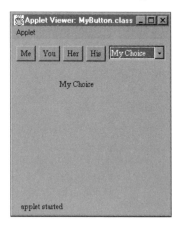

Figure 8.5: The MyButton applet displays the item that was selected from the list.

7 Experiment with the MyButton applet, and then terminate the applet.

ADDING A LIST CONTROL TO THE APPLET

Inside the init() method you added the following code:

```
Choice c;
```

In this code you declared a variable called *c* of type *Choice*. Then you used the addItem() method to add items to the list.

Now that the c variable has been declared, you can add it to the p panel:

```
p.add(c = new Choice());
```

The addItem() method can then be applied to add items to the c list:

```
c.addItem("My Choice");
  c.addItem("Her Choice");
  c.addItem("His Choice");
  c.addItem("Our Choice");
  c.addItem("Their Choice");
```

Now the list contains the following items:

```
My Choice
Her Choice
His Choice
```

```
Our Choice
Their Choice
```

DETECTING THE USER'S SELECTION FROM THE LIST

The action() method is used to determine if an item has been selected from the list:

```
public boolean action(Event evt, Object arg)
{

if (evt.target instanceof Choice)
    {
    sWhatWasPressed = (String)arg;
    }
else
    {
    ...
    ... Examine if a button was clicked
    ...
    }// end of else

...
...
...

}// end of action()
```

Note the use of the *if* statement, which examines whether or not an item from the list was selected:

```
if (evt.target instanceof Choice)
```

If the if statement is satisfied, it means that the user has selected an item from the list. The *arg* parameter represents the string of the selected item.

Quick Reference

O ne of the most important things about learning any programming
language is to know how to find information about the syntax of the language, the various ready-to-use methods that are supplied with the software, and other information relevant to the language. In short, to be able to use
a programming language, you must have an access to a good help mechanism
and a good reference material.

Getting help in Java

Popular compilers of modern programming languages (such as Visual Basic
and Visual C++) provide an on-screen help mechanism. This means that
while typing the code of your program you can press F1, for example, and a
Help window will open. This Help window will let you search for the particular subject that you need. This way, as you type your code, you can look up
how certain methods are spelled, what the parameters and returned values of
the methods are, and so on.

Currently, Java does not have its own text editor program for writing programs. (Recall that during the course of this book, you were instructed to type
Java code in a separate text editor, such as Notepad.) Nevertheless, Java does
have a help mechanism.

GETTING HELP FROM THE JAVA DOCUMENTATION

In Chapter 2 you were instructed to download the JDK from the Sun Web site. Another useful file that you can download from the Sun Web site is the documentation for Java.

To find out more about the API (Application Program Interface)—the methods of Java—download the JDK-1-0-apidocs.exe file from the Sun site. This self-extracting file contains a variety HTML documents that you can view with your Web browser. (You do not need to use a Java-enabled Web browser to view these files.) These files contain information about the various methods of Java.

Another reference file that you may find useful is the Programmer Guide for Java. This file also contains several HTML documents that you can view with your Web browser.

If you prefer, the JDK-beta2-psdocs.exe file on the Sun site contains all of the documents mentioned above in PostScript format. (Of course, to view PostScript files you need a program capable of reading this format.)

The API documentation and reference   The most useful documentation and reference that you'll find about Java is included with the API Documentation discussed above. Once you've downloaded and expanded this file, here's how to search for help with it.

First, open the AllNames.HTML file in your browser. (AllNames.HTML is one of the files that was extracted from the JDK-1-0-apidocs.exe file.) Note that you are viewing the HTML file locally on your hard drive; thus, the process of viewing the HTML pages is very fast. The AllNames.HTML page is shown in Figure R.1.

You can now scroll the page shown in Figure R.1 to look for a topic that you want to learn about. The topics are ordered alphabetically; clicking on one of the hypertext letters on the screen (A, B, C, and so on) takes you directly to subjects beginning with that letter of the alphabet. You may also want to manuever through this lengthy reference by using the Find (or Search) mechanism of your browser.

As an exercise, suppose that you are now writing a Java program and you want to find information about the drawString() method. Let's assume that you forgot what parameters you should supply to drawString() as well as the type of its returned value. Simply use the Search mechanism of your Web browser program to search for the word *drawString*. The section inside the AllNames.HTML page where the word *drawString* is mentioned is displayed as shown in Figure R.2.

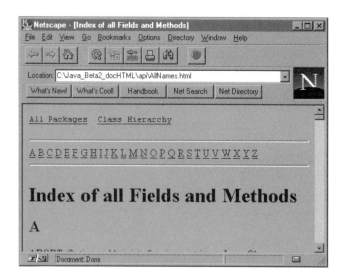

Figure R.1: The AllNames.HTML page

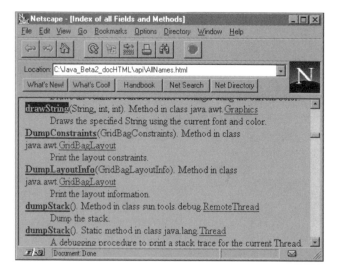

Figure R.2: Finding *drawString()* in AllNames.HTML

Note that the word *drawString* is hyperlinked. In some cases, the explanation displayed on the AllNames.HTML page is sufficient, but if you need more information, simply click the hyperlinked text.

Click on the *drawString()* hyperlink; the window shown in Figure R.3 appears explaining that the drawString() method takes three parameters and the returned value is void. The function of each of the parameters is also outlined on this page.

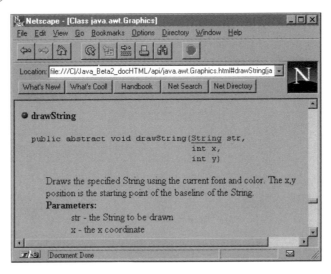

Figure R.3: Getting help on the drawString() method

Is the help mechanism in Java a useful one? As you can see, there is nothing wrong with the way you can search and hyperlink from one page to another; because the loading of the HTML pages is performed locally on your hard drive, the search is accomplished very fast.

GETTING HELP AND REFERENCE MATERIAL FROM THE DEMOS

Another good source of reference and help material is the sample applets supplied inside the C:\Java\Demo directory. Suppose that you found a method but you do not understand how to apply it in your program. The best way to see how to apply the method is to see it in action in one of the sample applets in C:\Java\Demo directory. To do this, use your word processor to load the *.java files of the sample applets, and then search for the method. If the method was used by one of the sample applets, you'll probably be able to understand how it works by looking at the *.java file in which it appears.

Because Java is still in its infancy, if you plan to be a Java developer, keep up with the latest releases of and discussions about the product by checking the Sun Web site and its many useful links frequently.

Index